Pride. Passion. Belief.

An England Fans' View of
EURO 2004

A Britespot Publication

PRIDE. PASSION. BELIEF.

It's the end of the domestic football season and inter-club rivalry has been temporarily cast aside. From Carlisle to Cornwall and Newcastle to Norwich, the flag of St George is proudly flying high.

Supermarkets are fast running out of beer as armchair supporters stock their fridges for the feast of football that is about to commence on our television screens and as many as 50,000 lucky England fans are slapping on the sunscreen in readiness for a summer in Portugal, host country of Euro 2004.

Such patriotism is nothing new to these shores when it comes to the England team competing in a major football tournament but the fanaticism this year seems to have scaled unprecedented heights.

Euro 2004 is a tournament that has gripped the nation like no other. Wherever you look white and red favours are fluttering in the early summer wind. Excitement is steadily building and an entire country is brimming with pride, passion and belief that this could be the year when England finally lay to rest the ghosts of 1966.

This unique publication tells the enthralling story of what happened next, from the perspective of the England fans who were involved, whether that be from the stands, the street, the pub or the sofa.

Without their contribution this publication would not have been possible and we thank everyone who took time out to submit their opinions or supply details of their experiences.

PridePassionBelief provided them with a platform to air their views on everything about the England team and Euro 2004, and collectively they have formed the only true, and most comprehensive, fans' record of events at the European Championships in Portugal.

We hope you enjoy the story they have to tell.

Foreword BY MALCOLM CLARKE

Malcolm Clarke has been Chair of the Football Supporters' Federation since its inception in 2002. He has been a match-going fan for nearly 50 years, and supports Stoke City, with a strong affiliation also to York City.

Firstly, I'd like to pass on the heartfelt thanks of all supporters who benefit from the work of the FSF to the staff, executive and members of Nationwide for their continued backing of the FSF.

The FSF is proud of the history it's inherited from its two founding partners, the National Federation of Football Supporters' Clubs and the Football Supporters' Association. In the case of the former, this goes back more than eighty years.

Our aim has been to forge a new organisation that draws on the very best from the past whilst also innovating and improving to give fans the voice they need and deserve in the modern game.

It may seem obvious but it's nevertheless worth repeating that there are two essential ingredients to professional football - players and fans. Without either there would be no professional game.

We aim to represent supporters' interests, provide services to them and to ensure that their views are not forgotten by those running the game.

We've worked very hard to create one united voice for fans, as was called for by the Government's Football Task Force. This has enabled us to extend our work with the England national side this year and we now regularly run "Fans' Embassies, continuing and extending our long-running work with the England national side.

As so many of you know, we ran our traditional "Fans' Embassy" service during Euro 2004 in Portugal – with the invaluable assistance of Nationwide who supported us throughout the England campaign. The Fan's Embassy was a massive success and helped many fans with issues in around the stadiums England played.

Although we did not manage to lift the Euro 2004 trophy-the fans definitely raised the roof with their support for England.

So, to you, the fans, I hope you enjoy reading about YOUR experiences of Portugal and continue to have the Pride, Passion and Belief in England. It's a beautiful game.

Malcolm Clarke
FSF Chair

An England Fans' View of

EURO 2004

First Published in Great Britain by
Britespot Publishing Limited
Chester Road, Cradley Heath, West Midlands B64 6AB

October 2004

© Britespot Publishing Limited

ISBN 1 904103 36 7

Cover design and layout
© *Britespot Publishing Limited*

Printed and bound in Italy

Acknowledgments
Britespot Publishing Limited would like to thank the following people who, without their invaluable assistance this publication would not have been possible. Nationwide Building Society - in particular Chris Hull, Paul Morris and Paul Hibbs, Malcolm Clarke of The Football Supporters' Federation, Sue Walsh and Jerry Werrett of givemefootball.com - the website of the Professional Footballers' Association, skysports.com, Glen Gibson of Jardine Communications and finally IntoFootball Limited.

Also Britespot Publishing Limited would like to thank the following fans' for their contributions which was also invaluable to the production of this publication. Mark Platt, Andy Garrard, Matt Miller, Nicki Wood, Paul Davies, David Burton, Geoffrey Howarth, Richard Godley, Andy Smith, Ben Bentley, Jonathan Owen, Daniel Gosling, Peter Stewart, Lee Payne, Aj Hennessey, Paul Underwood, Elliot Nicola, Robert Hawton, Nigel Phillips, Karen McCrudden, Ben Garside, Dawn Spooner, Bob Spittle, Caroline Dunn, Glenn Davis, Kim Dewdney, Sheena Chohan, Sharon Oliver, Carl Taylor, Keith Jones, Gary Collins, Stephen Hughes, Dominic Jackson, Tony Boulton, Adam Stanton, Iain Chiverton, Phil Hodgkinson, Adie Morris, Jason Devitt, Tim Wells, Manzar Akhter, Tony Westwood, Darren Smith, Collins Dokubo Owen, Andrew Deere, Mark Milne, Steven Barsby, David Brown, James Potten, Simon Peglar, Ian Trebilco, Paul Fisher, Alex Butcher, G Sing, Dawn Martin, Gerald Taylor, Alex Walke, Alan Lusher, Peter Dickinson, Chris Travis, Carl Hughes, Michael Heales, Darren Rodgers, Russell Stander, Dave Wheeler, Hass Khan, Jon Harvey, Craig Kent, Mike Eyre, Daniel Cook, Wayne McDowall, James Wills, Ben Fidge, John McKenzie, Terence Sheehan, Dan Smith, Bill Paul, Stuart Sale, Mark Egan, Matt Eccles, Philip Glaister, Richard Jones, Jamal Ahmed, James Creighton, Graham Hindle, Luong Tran, Simon Maurice, Paul Bridges, Mark Loveday, Harshil Parekh, James Brelsford, Mark Thompson, Ian Mccrory, Ian O'Neill, Ann Harvey, Darren Posnack, Richard McNally, Jim Pedley, Shahnawaz Hussain, Darrell Lamb, Kay Davies, Michael Jarrett, Colin Stein, Tamion von Christian, Trevor (Kopboyred) Lewis, Rob Dolphin, Jamie Foster, Simon Eland, Burnsie, Peeb, JJ, Emlyn Dudson, Clive Turner.

Contents PRIDE. PASSION. BELIEF.

HOW WE GOT THERE

Wherever you look white and red flags are fluttering in the early summer wind. Excitement is steadily building and an entire nation is brimming with pride, passion and belief that this could be the year when England finally lay to rest the ghosts of 1966...

The road to Portugal began in October 2002. Just a few months previous England had reached the last eight of the World Cup but alongside them in Group seven of the Euro qualifiers were Turkey, surprise semi-finalists in the Far East.

There was no doubt the head-to-head games between us would determine the winners of the group.

It was these fixtures that all England fans were looking forward to most but those two games apart, the qualifying campaign looked a pretty straightforward one.

Slovakia, Macedonia and Liechtenstein were not expected to put up too much of a fight, although each represented a trip to previously unchartered territory.

It all began on Saturday 12 October with an away win in Slovakia, but it was not as easy as expected and it was a match that set the tone for the rest of our group matches.

Middlesbrough's Slizard Nemeth opened the scoring for the hosts in front of a hostile home crowd in Bratislava and when the hour mark passed with no change in the score a major upset looked on the cards.

Thankfully, goals from Beckham and Owen eventually spared our blushes and ensured we got off to a winning start.

Macedonia were next up, at home. Nothing less than a straightforward three points were expected to be bagged but we ended the evening at Southampton's St Mary's Stadium grateful for a single point.

It was the night the curtain was finally drawn on the England career of the country's most famous ponytail.

A disappointing 2-2 draw signalled the end of David Seaman's international career. The keeper was at fault for at least one of the goals and it confirmed what the majority of us already knew.

With the memory of his blunder against Brazil still fresh in the mind these latest mishaps were the final straw. 'Safe Hands' was now not so and the time was right for a new number one.

It required a second half Steven Gerrard equaliser to spare our blushes but it was not enough to prevent barrage of criticism the following day.

According to the press, after just two games, our qualification hopes lay in tatters, the majority of players were not good enough and Sven was no longer the man to lead England into Euro 2004.

In situations like this an easy game is what you need. It's often said there are no easy games in international football but think of Liechtenstein and think again.

> "The Macedonia debacle confirmed what we'd all known for a long time and that was that David Seaman was well past his sell-by-date. He should have stepped down after the World Cup and it's sad that such an illustrious international career had to end this way." - Alex Charleston

This was the perfect fixture to raise morale and get back on track. Defeat here was unthinkable and, as the ridiculous odds that were on offer for a home win indicated, it was never going to happen. There are shocks in football but not even the most pessimistic of England fans was contemplating the horror defeat against the minnows would bring.

As expected, victory was achieved, although not in the emphatic manner that was anticipated.

Three points are three points, however, and after the Macedonian debacle we were grateful to return home with our reputation intact, Owen and Beckham netting again in low-key affair.

It was a result that set us up nicely for the big one. Turkey were due at the Stadium of Light four days later and everyone was up for this. A crackling atmosphere added to what was one of the most memorable England internationals of recent times and on a night of high tension a 76th minute strike from substitute Darius Vassell

and a last minute penalty by Becks sealed a crucial 2-0 win.

The outstanding performance of young Wayne Rooney was an added bonus, as was the world-class goalkeeping display by the much-maligned David James. We had control of the group and everything was looking all rosy once again.

The north-east was a happy hunting ground for Sven's men again when Slovakia visited these shores in the next qualifier. A goal from Janocko separated the sides at half-time but a second half revival, capped by a brace of goals from Mr Reliable Michael Owen, ensured relief swept around the Riverside Stadium.

With the 2003/04 season still in its infancy we then travelled to Macedonia on a revenge mission. Again we worryingly fell behind to a first half goal but another spirited second half fightback saw us take maximum points.

> "I've been following my county home and away since 1982 and I have to say the atmosphere in the Stadium of Light was the best I have ever known for a qualifying game involving England. It was absolutely electric and I've no doubt it contributed to what was an unforgettable victory." - Gerry Sonner

Rooney memorably notched his first international goal and the ever-dependable Becks secured victory via the spot.

The return with the part-timers from Liechtenstein provided a routine 2-0 win at Old

Chapter One HOW WE GOT THERE

Trafford, with the improving Rooney on the scoresheet again, this time with fellow Mersey star Owen.

It meant that with just one game to go we topped the group, one point ahead of Turkey, who just so happened to be our final opponents.

Almost a year to the day since our qualifying campaign began the day of destiny had arrived.

The stakes couldn't be higher in the volatile Ataturk Stadium, Istanbul. A draw would be good enough but everyone knew that playing for a point was a dangerous game to play.

As it turned out Sven's men turned in a highly professional performance and, just like the great European Cup winning Liverpool teams used to do, silenced the frenzied home crowd with a disciplined defensive display.

But for one of the worst penalty misses in living memory by David Beckham, we'd have returned home celebrating a glorious victory.

Thankfully, come the end of the night, it didn't matter and a gallant goalless draw was enough to assure us of qualification.

The distraught Turks were left facing the prospect of a dreaded two-legged play-off, while England fans looked ahead to a summer of sun, sand, sea and, hopefully, success in Portugal 2004.

This is our story…

Chapter Two ALL TOGETHER NOW

On 17 May and after months of speculation and debate the England squad for Euro 2004 is finally revealed. Twenty-three players made the final cut and it's basically those we expected. Some will agree with Sven's selection, some won't, but here they are — the men we are pinning our hopes on in Portugal and what we think of them...

David James (33 years old)
Goalkeeper with Manchester City

Now established as our undisputed number one after so long in the shadows of David Seaman, 'Jamo' has proved himself a dependable last line of defence for his country during a successful qualifying campaign in which he was an instrumental performer.

His outstanding displays against Turkey spring instantly to mind, with his miraculous late save at the Stadium of Light a particular highlight.

It was a stop the great Gordon Banks would have been proud of and the plaudits that came his way in the aftermath were fully deserved for a goalkeeper who is much improved in recent years.

Cruelly dubbed 'Calamity James' following a series of high-profile blunders in the past, the Man City stopper has certainly matured with

age and, as the oldest member of England's Euro 2004 squad, a lot of responsibility now rests on his broad shoulders.

This will be his first major tournament as the first choice England keeper and he'll be desperate to impress on the big stage.

With his huge athletic frame he cuts an imposing figure between the sticks and when it comes to shot stopping there's no doubt James is up there with the best of them.

But despite his size, many fans and commentators believe that he remains vulnerable at times when it comes to collecting crosses. So be prepared for some anxious moments when the ball is played into the heart of the England box.

He's received his fair share of criticism in the past but has worked hard to eradicate the deficiencies in his game and hopefully lapses of concentration by the big fella are now a thing of the past.

"David James is a keeper who's matured with age and despite some high-profile blunders earlier in his career he fully deserves to be England's number one in Portugal." - Steven Parr

Ian Walker (32 years old)
Goalkeeper with Leicester City

Ian Walker has never fulfilled the potential that once marked him down as a great England keeper of the future and is perhaps a touch fortunate to be on the plane to Portugal.

He won his first cap as long ago as 1996 but paid the price for allowing a Gianfranco Zola shot to slip through his grasp in an important World Cup qualifier against Italy at Wembley the following year. Loss of form for his club saw Walker fade from the international scene and it was only after helping Leicester gain promotion to the Premiership in 2003 that he was surprisingly welcomed back into the fold.

Ian has been called up to many squads since but has only added one further cap to his tally and has hardly excelled during a difficult season with relegated Leicester. But on the plus side, at 32 he's an experienced campaigner who shouldn't be phased if called upon.

"Deserves credit for resurrecting an international career that everyone thought was over. Had Chris Kirkland been fit it's doubtful Walker would have been selected, but good luck to him." - Gareth Symons

Paul Robinson (24 years old)
Goalkeeper with Tottenham Hotspur

Despite suffering relegation with Leeds, Robinson escaped with his reputation intact and the new Tottenham keeper will be keen to put a nightmare season behind him in Portugal.

Paul has long been regarded as one of the best young keepers in the country and his call-up to the Euro 2004 squad will give his confidence a welcome boost. He has limited experience on the international scene but is no stranger to big games, having performed impressively between the sticks during the Yorkshire club's run to the Champions League semi-final just a few years back.

Widely regarded as the understudy to David James, at 25, Robbo has time on his side to make a claim for the number one spot and Sven will have no worries about throwing him into the heat of the battle if need be.

"If he can't dislodge David James from the number one slot maybe he could be used as our emergency penalty taker, seeing as he scored a cracker from the spot for leeds earlier in the season." - Tony Peacock

Gary Neville (29 years old)
Defender with Manchester United

You certainly know what you're getting with Gary. Now a veteran of the England set-up, the eldest Neville brother will be a key player in Portugal. With over 60 caps to his name his experience will be crucial and we can ill-afford to be without him.

He seems to have been around the international scene for donkey's years and has seen off the challenge of many rivals for the right-back slot.

A true professional in every sense of the word, the Stretford End favourite may not win many popularity contests with opposition supporters in the Premiership but he commands the utmost respect for what he's achieved in the game.

Ashley Cole (23 years old)
Defender with Arsenal

A product of the Highbury youth system, Ashley has enjoyed a meteoric rise to stardom and is rightly regarded as one of this country's most talented young players.

The London-born defender has flourished under the guidance of Arsene Wenger at Arsenal, ousting Brazilian Silvinho from the left-back slot and never looking out of his depth in a star-studded side.

If one criticism could be levelled at him it would be that he can be a bit rash in the tackle at times. However, he more than makes up for this

Although they probably won't admit to it, most non Man United fans secretly harbour grudging admiration for Gary Neville. During a distinguished career at Old Trafford's he's seen and done it all and is among the most decorated individuals in Sven's squad.

All that is missing from his medal collection is an international honour of note. He was forced to miss the last World Cup through injury and will be aware that, at 29, time is running out to lift a trophy with the three lions on his chest.

"The England team just wouldn't seem the same without Gary Neville in it. He's an institution in that white shirt." - Sandra Neary

in other areas of his game. Blessed with electric pace, he loves to get forward at every opportunity and, with his eye-catching overlapping forays into opposition territory and accurate crossing, he offers an added attacking dimension.

Ashley excelled in the 2002 World Cup, where he figured in all five games for England and seems to have made the England left-back spot his own.

"Our best left full-back since Kenny Sansom, Coley has the potential to be one of the all-time greats and could be one of the big stars in Portugal."

- Brendan Gatesby

Jamie Carragher (26 years old)
Defender with Liverpool

Jamie was never considered a likely member of the Euro 2004 squad until late in the campaign but fully deserves his call-up.

One of the most improved players in the country, not much recognition comes his way but his value to Liverpool cannot be underestimated.

A no-nonsense defender who is equally adept at playing in both full-back positions or centre half, his versatility would be a big asset to any team. Strong in the tackle and an effective man-marker.

Has failed to establish himself as a regular member of the squad but would have gone to Japan two years ago had he not been required to undergo knee surgery.

A high level of consistency is another key attribute of his game but whether the rest of the squad (Gerrard and Rooney apart) can understand his broad accent remains to be seen!

"Not the greatest footballer in the world but definitely the one player in this squad I'd want alongside me in the trenches if the going got tough." - Steve Lindsay

John Terry (23 years old)
Defender with Chelsea

The English rock at the heart of the multi-national Chelsea defence, Terry has matured into one of the most accomplished centre backs in the country and has been touted as a potential England captain of the future.

A relative newcomer to Sven's squad, it was only twelve months ago that the Barking-born centre-back won his first full England cap against Serbia & Montenegro.

Has taken to international football like a duck to water and was instrumental in the Euro 2004 qualification clinching draw in Istanbul.

A natural leader, Terry possesses strength and composure in equal abundance, is dominant in the air and can play a bit too. Outstanding in Chelsea's run to the last four of the Champions League last season and has done an excellent job as skipper of the Blues in Desailly's absence.

Off-field problems resulted in him being overlooked for the World Cup in 2002 so he'll be hoping to make amends in this tournament and enhance his blossoming reputation further.

"John is your typical Cockney geezer and reminds me of a young Terry off Minder. A great player though, who is very much in the Tony Adams mould. If he gets his head down and continues to work hard I reckon he could turn out to be even better than big Tone, I rate him that highly." - Keith Welsh

Sol Campbell (29 years old)
Defender with Arsenal

A reassuring presence at the centre of any defence, big Sol will be the cornerstone of our defence in Euro 2004. A long time regular on the England scene, Campbell is vastly experienced and will be one of the first names on Sven's team sheet.

Like his Highbury team-mate Ashley Cole, he'll go into this tournament high on confidence after a unforgettable season at club level in which he played a key role in helping the Gunners go through an entire Premiership campaign without defeat.

The former Tottenham captain has gone from strength to strength since his highly controversial move across North London three years ago and, as a veteran of two European Championships and two World Cups, Campbell certainly won't be fazed by the big occasion.

Appeared in only four matches during the qualifying campaign for this tournament but was absolutely awesome in the all-important final match against the Turks in Istanbul.

> "Lose Sol and we're in trouble. I used to think he was overrated but not anymore. Proved himself at Arsenal and is our best defender without doubt." - Gerrard Tierney

Ledley King (23 years old)
Defender with Tottenham Hotspur

The most inexperienced member of our squad, and a surprise inclusion by Sven, the Tottenham youngster has emerged from nowhere this season to claim his place on the plane for Portugal.

Despite the troubles endured by Spurs in 2003/04, King can be well pleased with the level of his performances and was rewarded with a first full England cap against Portugal just months ago.

Ledley Joined Tottenham as a trainee in 1997, turning pro a year later, and has risen through the ranks to establish himself as one of the most highly-rated individuals at White Hart Lane. The friendly international in Portugal apart, he's relatively untried on the big stage though and it would represent a huge a gamble to throw him in from the start of Euro 2004.

> "The new Sol Campbell? Don't make me laugh! That's an insult to young Ledley who will prove to be a much better player. This tournament could be the making of him and I urge Sven to give him a chance, he won't disappoint."
>
> - Isiah Blakeman

Phil Neville (27 years old)
Defender with Manchester United

Will forever be associated with the part he played in our exit from Euro 2000. The late penalty he conceded against Romania in Holland four years ago led to the elimination of Kevin Keegan's side.

Like their kid, he's been around the international scene for a long time now and is one of our most experienced squad members. Has won a host of honours at club level and played in his share of big games.

Suffered the disappointment of missing out on the World Cup Finals in France and Japan/Korea so he'll be relieved to be in this time around.

Phil can play in either full-back position and, in recent seasons, has also proved himself a more than capable defensive midfield player. Such versatility is sometimes priceless in these big tournaments

"Lives in the shadow of his brother Gary but Phil is a top class professional in his own right, knows the game inside out and is a much better player than he's given credit for." - Davey Metcalf

Wayne Bridge (23 years old)
Defender with Chelsea

An exciting, attacking, left-back who enjoyed an excellent first season at Stamford Bridge, where he slotted in with ease among the multitude of big name superstars brought to the club.

Went to Japan for the World Cup two years ago and enjoyed a brief taste of the action against Argentina. Not yet an automatic first choice in the number three shirt though but is pushing Ashley Cole hard.

Gained some vital big match experience playing for Chelsea in the Champions League last season and proved he can rise to the occasion, not least in the all-English quarter-final against Arsenal when he struck the all-important winner.

Bridge is rapidly developing into a top class player and he'd be an automatic starter for most other sides in the finals. If required he could also be an option on the left of midfield.

"One of the most consistent performers at the Bridge last season, Wayne is like a young Maldini! As a Shed regular for over 20 years I may be a touch bias but I firmly believe he should be given the nod over Ashley Cole when it comes to playing left-back for England." - Barry Sidwell

Nicky Butt (29 years old)
Midfielder with Manchester United

Not good enough for United but good enough for England. That's the frustrating predicament Nicky Butt has found himself in. Sir Alex has virtually deemed Butt surplus to requirements at Old Trafford.

It's a different story on the international front though where he remains very much part of England's plans. Sven is a big fan of the combative Mancunian and he could well see more action in the white shirt of England this summer than he has done in the red of United.

He surprised a lot of people by playing a starring role at the World Cup in Japan and always seems to do well when representing his country.

Can occupy the midfield holding role with good effect and if the diamond formation is employed then there'll be a lot of support for him to start.

"Not many people will be excited by the inclusion of Nicky Butt in the squad but against flair teams such as France I would start with him every time.." - Stuart Fielding

Steven Gerrard (24 years old)
Midfielder with Liverpool

Arguably, one, if not the finest midfielder in Europe at the moment, Stevie G's all-round game has improved so much that he's now considered as important as Beckham and Owen.

Had he been playing in a successful team last season Gerrard would have given Thierry Henry a run for his money in the Footballer of the Year awards. He's been that good.

His performances have been of such a consistently high standard that Alex Ferguson has earmarked him as the ideal candidate to replace Roy Keane. Truth is, he's a better player already. An all-action powerhouse of a player who dominates games and covers every blade of grass, Gerrard is the driving force in the England midfield.

Until recently he'd never been on the losing side for his country in a senior international. Unfortunately, Sweden put paid to that lucky omen in March but his mere presence in the side is enough to inspire those around him.

"Zidane? Figo? Nedved? Nah, you can keep them all. None of them can touch our Stevie. An inspirational captain of Liverpool who should be given the armband for England as well. A true leader in every sense of the word. Should emerge from Euro 2004 as one of the best players in the world." - Richie Legg

Owen Hargreaves (23 years old)
Midfielder with Bayern Munich

Born in Canada, lives in Germany and plays for England, Owen Hargreaves' background is far from that of your typical England international but his commitment when playing for his father's homeland cannot be faulted.

An energetic and combative midfielder, who can also slot in as an emergency right-back, Hargreaves is highly valued by Sven.

Steady rather than spectacular, the Bayern Munich man was a European Cup winner with the Bavarian giants in 2001 and earned a call-up to the senior England squad as a result.

A highly regarded player in the Bundesliga, if rumours are to be believed he could be on his way to the Premiership soon and he'll be eager to impress watching scouts in Euro 2004.

> "Something of an unknown quantity because he's never played in the Premiership, the fact that he's so highly regarded at such a club as Bayern Munich confirms that he's a talented player" - Brian Jameson

Frank Lampard (26 years old)
Midfielder with Chelsea

Has blossomed into one of the most accomplished and respected midfield players in England during 2003/04 and overshadowed Chelsea's big name foreign imports in the process.

The fact he was runner-up only to Thierry Henry in the PFA Player of the Year awards for 2003/04 is proof of the improvement in his game.

A tireless midfield worker, Lampard possesses a fine range of passing and keen eye for goal. When called upon by England in the past he hasn't let his country down but is a lot more effective as an attacking midfielder rather than a defensive one.

A former England under-21 captain, he won his first full cap against Belgium five years ago and has since gradually established himself as a regular in the squad.

After missing out on Euro 2000 and the World Cup of two years later he'll be chomping at the bit to test himself against Europe's finest in Portugal and the time is right for him to be given that chance.

> "Lamps is a must for a place in Sven's starting eleven at Euro 2004. Him and Gerrard together in the centre of midfield is a mouth-watering prospect and one good enough to take on the best in Europe." - Jim Corbett

David Beckham (29 years old)
Midfielder with Real Madrid

Golden balls. Our captain and the man we are pinning our hopes on most.

His first season with Real may not have turned out as glorious as he would have hoped in terms of silverware but there can be no doubt that playing alongside his fellow Los Galacticos has broadened his horizons and added more to his game.

His reign in Spain may not have been without controversy but he's settled well on the pitch and shone alongside Figo, Zidane, Ronaldo and company. He has matured immensely since taking over the England captaincy and has developed into an inspirational leader.

There won't be many better strikers of a dead ball in Portugal than Becks that's for sure and any set-piece in or around the opposition penalty box will have us on the edge of our seats in anticipation, while his pinpoint crossing from the right will provide the service our strikers thrive on.

"If Becks is a good as we are led to believe then he'll grab this tournament by the scruff of the neck and lead England to victory. I've no doubt about his ability, I just hope he can stay focussed and bury the ghosts of France 98" - Alex Goodway

Kieron Dyer (25 years old)
Midfielder with Newcastle United

Doubts continue to surround the fitness of Dyer and for this reason more than a few eyebrows were raised about his selection in the squad.

Ability-wise there'd be no questions asked about his inclusion.

If fully fit Dyer can take these finals by storm but injuries have unfortunately, once again, blighted his season.

Apart from the odd flashes of brilliance he's failed to live up to his reputation and now is the time for him to deliver in an England shirt. An exciting talent who will be looking to shed his injury prone tag.

A skilful, speedy player with seemingly unlimited reserves of energy and an eye for goal, Dyer has a lot to prove in Portugal.

"Dyer has the potential to be a major star at Euro 2004 so long as he stays free from injury and is given a chance in the team" - Robbie Cushion

Joe Cole (22 years old)
Midfielder with Chelsea

Without doubt one of the most technically gifted individuals in the current squad, Joe Cole is an enigmatic talent who can elate and frustrate in equal measure.

Poses a threat whenever on the ball and his twinkle-toed trickery is a delight to watch. A graduate of the West Ham academy, this young Cockney has improved and matured as a player since moving to Chelsea, despite often falling victim to the club's infamous rotation policy.

Joe has been spoken about as an England star of the future since his schoolboy days and has had to live with the burden that comes with the hype ever since.

Was the youngest member in our squad for the 2002 World Cup and made just one appearance.

> "If he was Brazilian, Joe Cole would be hailed as one of the greatest players in the world. His talent is not fully appreciated in this country and it's a shame because when it comes to skilful players he's right up there with the best of them." - Julie Rydale

Paul Scholes (29 years old)
Midfielder with Manchester United

Our most prolific goalscoring midfielder since David Platt, Scholesy may have endured a rare barren spell in front of goal for his country during the qualifying campaign but he's always one of the first names that come to mind when contemplating a good value first goalscorer bet.

An England regular for seven years now, the ginger haired Mancunian is an integral member of Sven's first choice eleven. Was an ever-present in the last World Cup and, even when he's not popping up to score vital goals, his value to the team is immense.

Like his fellow Manchester United team-mates in the current England set-up Scholes is a highly decorated player with a wealth of experience when it comes to playing in big games.

Originally a forward, he has an uncanny ability to be in the right place at the right time, timing his runs from midfield to perfection and netting in important games, a trait that was once the trademark of another Old Trafford and England legend, Bryan Robson.

> "He'll get a goal in Portugal, I'd put my mortgage on it. Such an intelligent player, an unsung hero who deserves to bracketed alongside the likes of Figo and Zidane. One of our most valuable players without doubt." - Kieron Ward

Emile Heskey (26 years old)
Forward with Birmingham City

A regular member of Sven's England squad, Heskey is by no means the deadliest of strikers, in fact his goals return is disappointing, but his ability to play out wide on the left as well as up front is a useful asset, while he's appreciated by his team-mates for his unselfishness and the work he does off the ball.'

A cup treble winner in 2001 with Liverpool the former Leicester star has recently returned to the Midlands after moving to Birmingham and hopefully this new start will help him reproduce the type of form that once persuaded Gerard Houllier to fork out £11 million for him.

> Heskey has his fair share of critics but Sven sees something in him that the most in the stands don't and that is a view we must respect" - Terry Hales

Wayne Rooney (18 years old)
Forward with Everton

Still only 18, the potential of this boy is frightening. Quite simply, he's the most exciting teenage talent in world football and we thank God that he's English!

Blessed with a devastating mix of pace, strength and skill, Rooney burst onto the scene as a 16-year old fresh from the Everton youth team and immediately began rewriting the record books. His adoring fans at Goodison quickly christened him 'Roo-naldo' and the comparisons with the Brazilian superstar were not over the top.

In February 2003, at the tender age of 17 years and 111 days, he became the youngest full England international when he appeared as a second half substitute against Australia.

When he netted his first goal for the Three Lions away at Macedonia in September that same year he became this country's youngest

international goalscorer and experienced hacks were running out of superlatives to describe him.

Euro 2004 will represent the biggest test of his young career to date. His critics may argue that he's still a bit rough around the edges and inexperienced when it comes to performing on the big stage but as Pele proved in 1958, when he took the World Cup by storm aged just 17, age is no barrier if you're good enough and Rooney has the ability to do likewise in Portugal.

> "As an Evertonian I'll be watching him in Portugal with mixed emotions. Naturally I want the lad to do well and fire England to glory but if he has a good tournament all the top clubs will be knocking on Moysie's door with an open cheque book and Everton cannot afford to lose him." - Mary McDowell

Michael Owen (24 years old)
Forward with Liverpool

St Etienne '98, Munich '01 and Japan '02, Michael is a man for the big occasion and can be relied upon to do the business when it matters most.

His strike rate in a Three Lions shirt is a mightily impressive one – averaging just under a goal every other game. He's gradually climbing up the list of all-time England goalscorers and has the potential to surpass the achievements of record goal-getter Bobby Charlton.

A genuine world-class striker, he remains our most likely goal threat and opposition defenders will be having nightmares about how to deal with his blistering pace, tricky feet and phenomenal eye for goal. Sprung to national consciousness with THAT goal against Argentina in the 1998 World Cup and has been the number one choice to lead the England attack ever since. His hat-trick in the unforgettable 5-1 thrashing of Germany was one of the great England moments of all-time.

"If Owen is on top form and banging the goals in I genuinely believe we could go all the way. Ignore his recent club form. There won't be many better strikers out in Portugal and he'll strike fear into the opposition." - Joshua Rowntree

Darius Vassell (24 years old)
Forward with Aston Villa

Vassell held off strong claims from Jermaine Defoe to win the last striking berth in the 23-man squad for Euro 2004.

The Aston Villa forward celebrated his full England debut in February 2002 by netting the only goal of a creditable 1-1 draw against Holland in Amsterdam.

He followed that up by coming off the bench to open the scoring in the vital home win over Turkey in the qualifying campaign for Euro 2004.

He seems totally at ease when playing at international level and showed no sign of nerves at the last World Cup where he made three appearances as England reached the last eight.

Remarkably Darius can boast a more prolific scoring record for his country than his club and is at his most effective for England when coming into the game as a substitute. Could be our secret weapon in Portugal.

"Has proved himself in an England shirt and, like Gary Lineker at the Mexico World Cup in 1986, this tournament could catapult him to stardom" - Tracey Castle

Chapter Three GETTING IT RIGHT

Now we know the squad for Portugal the guessing game begins as to which players will make it into Sven's starting eleven for the opening game of Euro 2004...

The Problem in Goal

Barring injury, David James will keep goal for England in Portugal. True, James is the best around right now and he's enjoyed a decent season. But he's hardly the reassuring presence between the sticks that you expect from an England keeper, as supporters of Liverpool, Aston Villa, West Ham and now Manchester City will testify.

Gone are the days when the England manager had five or six top class custodians to choose from and had James been playing twenty years earlier then his inclusion in the full squad would be very much in doubt.

How Sven must wish he could turn the clock back to the late seventies/early eighties.

The days when England produced the best goalkeepers in the world and Ron Greenwood could choose from such goalkeeping greats as Peter Shilton, Ray Clemence, Joe Corrigan and Jimmy Rimmer.

Had it not been for injury Liverpool's Chris Kirkland would have been almost certain of joining James in the squad for Portugal. Whether he'd have managed to oust the City stopper from the number one slot we'll never know but he'd have had strong claims to be the number two, at least, with Ian Walker more than likely being the man to have made way. Suspension and injuries have severely weakened

our defensive wall and any more setbacks in this area could severely jeopardise our chances of success out in Portugal.

> "David James has proved to be the best in England, that is without doubt. To be the best in England means you get picked for the England team- follow these simple steps and you realise that we don't have a problem in goal." - James Brelsford

> "It's time for new blood between the sticks and Paul Robinson has all the tools neccesary to make him England's number one for many years to come. He is easily our best keeper and at just 24 years old has time on his side" - Emlyn Dudson

> "What a pity Chris Kirkland is injured. He's the most promising young keeper this country has produced for donkey's years and would be my undisputed first choice between the sticks if fit."
>
> - Richard McNally

> "Banks, Shilton and Seaman, possibly the 3 greatest England goalkeepers ever. Are we, as England fans, expecting too much of the new goalkeepers? And is the pressure put on them, leading to blunders in goal? Some will say experience may be the best bet and that James or Walker will instil confidence in our defence but maybe to pick a younger goalkeeper, like Robinson, is the best bet. He's a proven shot stopper and in my opinion, the best England keeper." - Matt Miller

> "We have some excellent young talent surfacing and there will be fierce competition for that number one shirt. All I can say is it's time to give the likes of Paul Robinson and Chris Kirkland a proper chance!" - Mark Milne

The Defensive Wall

Rio Ferdinand's ban is a massive blow. Had he been available it would have been him and big Sol at the heart of the back four. The pair looked to have been forging a great understanding and would have been formidable together.

Alas, it was not to be and the hunt as been on to see who will take Rio's place.

Middlesbrough's Gareth Southgate looked to be the obvious option at one time until injury prematurely curtailed his season. Newcastle's Jonathon Woodgate was another possibility until he suffered a similar fate, leaving Chelsea's John Terry out on his own as the main candidate for a place alongside Sol.

Terry comes into this tournament on the back of a fine season at club level, has the necessary

attributes to the job and is now seen as the ideal choice to fill Rio's boots.

Should Terry or Campbell suffer injury or loss of form in the finals then we could be in trouble. Jamie Carragher and Ledley King provide the back up for our centre backs.

Carra only came into the reckoning late on and has played the majority of his club football at full-back, while King has bags of potential but lacks experience on the international stage.

The two full-back positions are slightly less complicated. Gary Neville will play right-back, there's no arguments there. The United stalwart is one of the most experienced defenders in Europe and is without doubt the best option we have to play in this position. On the left Ashley Cole will be favourite to start but his selection is not as clear-cut and Chelsea's

Wayne Bridge is breathing down his neck for a place in the starting line-up. Both are good attacking full-backs but Cole probably deserves to be given the nod for what he has achieved at Highbury last season.

Other full-back options include Phil Neville, Jamie Carragher and Owen Hargreaves, three players for whom the tag 'jack of all trades' could well apply.

"Even with Rio Ferdinand and Jonathan Woodgate missing we still have one of the best defences in Euro 2004. Sol Campbell is fast becoming the new Tony Adams and John Terry just keeps getting better with each game" - Al Hope

"I think the partnership of Campbell and King in defence seems to work just right and I would play Terry as the sweeper." - Robert Hawton

"Who'll partner Sol is the question on everyone's lips and my preference would be to move Gary Neville into the centre and play Jamie Carragher at right back. Neville has played in that position with good effect for United and is experienced enough to adapt, while Carragher is a solid stopper who's had an impressive season." - Michael Seddon

"I'd be much more confident of chances in Portugal if Sven had his first choice defence to choose from. But it's not to be and we just have to get on with it. Ferdinand, Woodgate and Southgate's misfortune could well pave the way for a new defensive star to emerge." - Stuart Pike

Options In Midfield

It is in this area of the pitch that we are probably at our strongest. In Beckham, Gerrard and Scholes, Sven has three world-class performers at his disposal who would walk into the starting line-up of every other team in Portugal.

Lampard is not far behind them and if we're going to select our strongest starting eleven he would make up the midfield quartet, unless Sven opts for the diamond formation. Then Lamps may have to be sacrificed for Nicky Butt. But if we go with four across the middle, in a traditional 4-4-2 formation, then Beckham, Gerrard, Lampard and Scholes is surely the best option.

For the quality of his crossing you'd go with Becks on the right. His understanding with right-back Gary Neville and ability to deliver pinpoint crosses into the heart of the opposition danger-zone makes him the obvious choice for this position.

In the centre Gerrard and Lampard could potentially form a devastating partnership, their styles complimenting each other perfectly, with both equally adept at launching into attack and getting back to shield the defence.

That would leave Scholes to occupy the problem position on the left. Not his natural position but one that will give him the freedom he craves. The strength in depth of our midfield will be the envy of most other nations and it's reassuring to know that there are numerous options at Sven's disposal should he feel the need to chop and change.

As well as Nicky Butt, Phil Neville and Jamie Carragher can play the midfield holding role should a more defensive approach be required, while, offensively, Kieron Dyer offers a different attacking dimension down the flanks, Joe Cole, with his bag of tricks, has the ability to take any opposition by surprise and Owen Hargreaves can slot into virtually whatever position he is asked to.

"My feelings about our midfield are that, Steven Gerrard can win the tournament for us if he is allowed to express himself more by not having the defensive shackles on him. I have seen him play both roles for Liverpool but the one he plays best is as an offensive player not defensive. He should also be given the captains armband as he is a born leader." - Peter Dickinson

"The days have gone since England boasted the likes of John Barnes, Tom Finney and Ray Kennedy. The later never actually played in a World Cup which shows that England have never been blessed on the left. People continually dream of Ryan Giggs running down the wing for England or even think if only Pires was English. However we have to cope with what we have." - Ben Bentley

"The midfielder who I thought should've gone to Portugal was Gareth Barry. He had an exceptional season on the left of midfield for Aston Villa, and there ain't no other English players who have had a better season. The other plus factor about Gareth is that he could've slotted into defence without any problems. If you're going to use a flat 4 in midfield you need to use a natural left footer on the left wing which Paul Scholes ain't." - Carl Taylor

"The diamond formation does not work as it leaves two players out of position, Frank Lampard holding and Steven Gerrard out on the left of the four. This pair were arguably two of the best three players in the Premiership season, trailing Thierry Henry. However, in this flat midfield, Gerrard and Lampard are in the centre where they belong and where they can influence the game.

The other midfielders in England's squad have different strengths. Owen Hargreaves is an excellent player but he is better in the centre rather than on the left-hand side where he is usually brought on. He is a starter for Bayern Munich and has a great shot and cross on him, and he is also versatile. So is Phil Neville, but that, in my opinion, is his only strength. I don't think he offers the team anything and I still wonder why he is picked every time. Kieron Dyer and Joe Cole are potential match-winners but never seem able to produce the goods. - Alex Butcher.

"We need to use naturally left-footed players on the left hand side. Why we refuse to give Bridge and Cole another shot together I do not know. It worked before (against Macedonia) even if we did only draw." - Ian Trebilco

"I don't envy anyone who plays in midfield but I can proudly say we have a line-up in midfield that would make it into any fantasy football team! Probably the best selection of players in the world, with the likes of Beckham who has matured into a true leader and superstar and can drop a ball on a five pence piece from 60 yards. Scholes who can unleash a shot to terrorise any goalkeeper, Lampard whose move to Chelsea has proved how valuable a team player he really is and Gerrard who can leave the opposing midfield in his wake when he goes on one of his infamous runs. Up the Wolves!" - Peeb

The Striking Blend

The decision to go with just four strikers is a slightly worrying one and few other teams will travel to Portugal with such limited resources in attack.

Jermaine Defoe and Alan Smith were originally in the reckoning to make the squad but ultimately overlooked and by not taking an extra forward our options look a little threadbare to say the least.

Supposing we go with the tried and trusted two up front. You can't go into a major tournament without one of the most feared strikers in Europe, so that's Michael Owen's place in the starting eleven assured.

We can only shudder to think what we'll do if our number ten gets injured.

But if he can stay fit and reproduce the form that has already made him a national hero then defences of Europe beware.

The big question then is who will partner him in attack?

Emile Heskey is the most experienced of the remaining trio and has the advantage of having played alongside Owen for Liverpool and England regularly over the past four years.

However, as a striking partnership they have hardly set the world alight and the fact that Heskey scores so few goals means the goalscoring burden falls too heavily on Owen.

Darius Vassell has produced the goods when pulling on an England shirt in the past. Added to that, he not used to starting games for England and has proved to be more effective when used as a sub.

That leaves young Wayne Rooney. Forget his age. If he's good enough, he's old enough. Rooney is fearless and will be chomping at the bit to test himself against such world-renowned defenders the likes of Desailly, Stam and Nesta.

You can be sure that if the Italians, the French, the Germans or the Spaniards, to name just four of the competing nations, had such a precocious talent in their ranks they would play him. We must do the same.

What is the point of hold back a player of his vast potential? This tournament could elevate him into the world superstar he's tipped to become so let's give him that chance.

Rooney and Owen are our two best forwards without a doubt. Pair them together and let them fire England to Euro glory.

"We have some really great strikers, like Wayne Rooney and Michael Owen, but we also have some new generation attackers also, like Jermaine Defoe and Darius Vassell. All Sven needs to do now is find the right combination of strikers, like Rooney partnering Vassell or Owen with Defoe." - Lee Payne

Chapter Three GETTING IT RIGHT

"Up front we are playing Owen for what he has done in the past and not his current form. We would be much better having Darius Vassell up there, because he always performs for England and is much more of a goal threat. Wayne Rooney has everything strength, pace, power, skill and a great eye for goal. He will be a great player for England for many years to come." - Andrew Deere.

"England do have some really good strikers, like Wayne Rooney and Michael Owen, but we also have some new generation attackers as well, like Jermaine Defoe and Darius Vassell. All Sven needs to do now is find the right combination of strikers, like Rooney partnering Vassell or Owen with Defoe." - Lee Payne

As an England fan, we seem to put more pressure on our national team strikers to deliver more than any other nation in the world. This, I have to say, is unfair considering the amount of foreign players that make up our domestic league. Although we have the best league in the world, a lot of the teams' strikers are there so our domestic teams can compete in Europe. The game has evolved so much over the past ten years it is rare to have a combination such as Greaves and Hurst upfront. Saying that, when Owen burst on the scene with the aging Shearer, we thought we would make it all the way once again. In our current squad, I hope our star players that are privileged enough to wear the three lions work together rather than battle as individuals. With Rooney's strength, Owen prowling round the box and Heskey delivering, we should see an England team to build on for the future. Come on England! - Burnsie

"Alan Smith would have been one of the first names in my squad. He has the fire in his belly that every England player should possess." - Jason Devlin

Chapter Three GETTING IT RIGHT

"Michael Owen and Wayne Rooney have to be one of the greatest striking partnerships of any international team, however I am personally worried about the possibility of either of these two getting injured or suspended. We don't have a third top class quality striker, whereas the French have Saha, the Spanish Torres, and we only have the likes of Heskey and Vassell, who are not on a par with the likes of Saha or Torres. This is my concern, as I cannot see Vassell or especially Emile Heskey scoring us a goal to win a match when we get to the final rounds of Euro 2004. Should England have brought someone along the likes of James Beattie to give us that variety up front? Personally I'm not sure, but all I can say is I hope Michael and Wayne stay fit." - Paul Davies

"Picking two out of four is the key, but which two? Do you go for form or past reputation? Many fans like to keep with Owen and Rooney, some would change Owen for Vassell. Personally keeping with Owen and Rooney gives an even balance and with these two enables a long batting innings with potentially another four tournaments together. So all we need now is an umbrella and a cheery on a stick. The perfect cocktail." - Darren Rodgers

Our Perfect XI (playing to a 4-4-2 formation)

Wayne Rooney (Striker)   **Michael Owen** (Striker)

Paul Scholes (Left midfield)   **Steven Gerrard** (Centre midfield)   **Frank Lampard** (Centre midfield)   **David Beckham** (Right midfield)

Ashley Cole (Left-Back)   **John Terry** (Centre-back)   **Sol Campbell** (Centre-back)   **Gary Neville** (Right-back)

David James (Goalkeeper)

How we rate our rivals for the Euro 2004 crown... Starting with our Group B opponents

France

Reigning European Champions and almost everybody's pre-tournament favourites, our rivalry with the French goes back centuries and is not confined solely to football.

With the flair players France have in their team there's no denying they are a joy to watch. We know all about the quality of Henry, Pires, Vieira, Desailly and company, and it's no surprise that, the 2002 World Cup apart,

Player to beware: Thierry Henry

they have been the dominant force in international football for the past six years. The only country to qualify for Portugal with a one hundred per cent record, they are aiming to become the first nation to successfully defend the European crown.

To face them in the opening game is not ideal but if we want to win Euro 2004 we'll have to beat the best, so let's get on with it.

Croatia

Although not the force they once were, the 1998 World Cup semi-finalists still possess some quality players in their squad and are capable of producing an upset or two in Portugal.

New Rangers striker Dado Prso will lead their attack and he proved in last season's Champions League with Monaco that he can

Player to beware: Dado Prso

score goals on the big stage. At the back Juve's Igor Tudor has a big reputation but their midfield is considered weak and their first choice goalkeeper has been ruled out with injury.

Our game with Croatia in Lisbon on June 21 could be crucial to our hopes of progression and they won't be an easy touch.

Switzerland

Considered the soft touch in our group but the Swiss won't roll over, as we discovered in Euro '96 when they were the party poopers in our opening game on home soil.

Qualified impressively from a group that included Ireland and Russia but we expect to

Player to beware: Hakan Yakin

take nothing less than maximum points from them when we meet in Coimbra on 17 June.

Their squad contains a couple of talented youngsters but still relies too much on the ageing captain Stephane Chapuisat who, at 35, is past his sell-by-date.

Group A

Portugal

The weight of expectation that comes with being the host nation often proves too much of a burden and this Portuguese team has a lot to live up to.

Their so-called 'golden generation' are close to their sell-by-date and Euro 2004 represents their last chance of success. Figo and co have never had a better chance of glory but can they live with the pressure?

Player to beware: Cristiano Ronaldo

Apart from having to face Spain in the opening round of group games the draw was kind to Portugal and with the ability they have they should progress to the latter stages at least.

However, they've have never gone beyond the semi-final stage in a major tournament so history will have to be made if they are to become the first nation to win the European Championships on home soil since France 20 years ago.

Spain

The great under-achievers of international football. We think we've had it tough going 38 years without a major trophy. Well the Spaniards have had to wait even longer and almost every tournament they enter they do so with high hopes of success.

European champions on home soil in 1964 and runners-up in France two decades later the

Player to beware: Raul

Portuguese climate will suit Spain and they go into Euro 2004 as one of the fancied teams.

Too often in the past they have shown a tendency to self-destruct on the big stage but will definitely be one of the teams to look out for and with their fans not having far to travel they'll be strongly backed to finally fulfil expectations.

Russia

Despite breaking Welsh hearts in the play-off for Euro 2004, Russia are not expected to make a serious impact in Portugal.

Their squad is not the strongest and their preparations for Euro 2004 have been hit by injury and suspension to key players.

Player to beware: Dmitri Bulykin

As a nation, the Russians are no strangers when it comes to participating in major tournaments but not a lot is expected of them in Portugal.

It's hard to see them upsetting either the hosts or Spain and they face a tall order to progress into the knockout phase.

Greece

The Greeks don't have a good track record when it comes to competing in major tournaments. They are yet to win a game and are not expected to change that habit in Euro 2004

Defensively very strong, Greece lack punch in attack and could well be prepared to sit back and adopt spoiling tactics.

Player to beware: Giorgios Karagounis

Did well to qualify when you consider they lost their opening two games and the fact that they topped the group ahead of Spain means they are no mugs but it will be a big surprise if they come through the group stage.

If they do then we wouldn't mind meeting them in the quarter-final, that's for sure!

Group C

Italy

You can guarantee the Italians will be there or there about when the latter stages of the Euro Championships or World Cup comes around.

The Azzurri were just 13 seconds away from success in Euro 2000 and they'll be hell-bent on avenging that agonising final defeat to France. With their renowned rock solid defence

Player to beware: Francesco Totti

superbly marshalled by Nesta and Cannavaro, and players of such quality as Totti and Del Piero pulling the strings at the opposite end there's no doubt they have the talent to go all the way in Portugal. World Champions on three occasions, Italy last triumphed in the European Championship 36 years ago but are deservedly rated as one of the favourites for Euro 2004.

Denmark

Shock winners of this tournament 12 years ago.

Denmark know what is required to go all the way but their current squad lacks the class of that what won Sweden '92 and qualification from the group stage will be viewed as a success this time around.

Player to beware: Martin Jorgensen

Having beaten us 3-2 at Old Trafford not long ago we know more than most what the Danes are capable of but they'd hold no fears for Sven's men should we meet again in the latter rounds of Euro 2004. Newcastle flop Jon Dahl Tomasson is their main goal threat and that says it all really.

Sweden

The Swedes have been boosted by the return of Celtic legend Henrik Larsson and they'll fancy their chances of progressing from the group stage.

Infamously ended our hopes in Euro '92, when they reached the last four. But that was on home soil and they have never gone beyond the semi-final in the European Championships.

Bulgaria

The golden age of Bulgarian football is well and truly over. The legendary Hristo Stoichkov has long retired and memories of USA '94, when they upset the odds to reach the last four, are fading fast.

Fans of Liverpool and Manchester United will have heard of Dimitar Berbatov, a member of

Group D

Holland

So often their own worst enemies, Holland are capable of going far in Portugal but only if their efforts are not undermined by unrest in the camp that has plagued them in previous tournaments. With a richly talented squad the Dutch no doubt have the ability to repeat their glorious triumph of 1988. The mere mention of

Player to beware: Zlatan Ibrahimovic

It'll be a major surprise if they get that far in Portugal and if they do the Abba records will have to be dusted down in celebration back in Sven's homeland.

The exciting Ajax striker Zlatan Ibrahimovic could be their secret weapon, while Arsenal's Freddie Ljungberg will also be a key player.

Player to beware: Dimitar Berbatov

the Bayer Leverkusen side that reached the Champions League Final a couple of years back, while Stilian Petrov is a firm favourite north of the border with Celtic.

But them apart, the Bulgarian squad is relatively inexperienced and not a lot is expected of them in Portugal.

Player to beware: Ruud Van Nistelrooy

players such as Kluivert, Davids, Van Nistelrooy and Van der Vaart is enough to strike fear into the opposition and they'll be a formidable force if they can remain focussed on the task in hand.

Drawn in a tough group but if they can come through that they'll have a good a chance.

THE OPPOSITION

Germany

Never write off the Germans. This must be one of the most overused clichés in football, but it's true. Champions of Europe on three previous occasions they have the uncanny knack of rising to the occasion in major tournaments no matter how good or bad their form is.

No-one gave our age old rivals a chance at the last World Cup but they defied the odds to

Player to beware: Michael Ballack

reach the final and love them or loathe them you have to respect Germany for what they've achieved.

No Englishman needs reminding of the hurt they inflicted on us at Wembley eight years ago but we managed to beat them in the last Euro finals and we'll certainly fancy our chance if we meet again in Portugal.

Czech Republic

Qualified impressively for these finals and should not be underestimated in Portugal. Always seem to be labelled the dark horses but the way the Czech's performed in the qualifiers they deserve to be bracketed among the favourites for Euro 2004.

Impressively swept aside the challenge of Holland on route to these finals and can boast

Player to beware: Milan Baros

some of the most technically gifted European players in their squad.

In Pavel Nedved they possess the continent's reigning footballer of the year, while Liverpool's Milan Baros and Borussia Dortmund's Tomas Rosicky are youngsters of enormous potential. They are capable of going far but could have peaked too soon.

Latvia

Competing in their first ever tournament, the Latvians are the rank outsiders and to be honest we know very little about them.

Proved their pedigree by beating Turkey in the play-offs but were the team everyone in the tournament wanted to be grouped with

Player to beware: Marian Pahars

when the draw for Euro 2004 was made. Regarded as a dour side who hit teams on the break they're not expected to make any impact in Portugal.

It will be a major achievement if they pick up a single point.

Chapter Five

WARM UP GAMES

The Summer Tournament (1st - 5th June 2004)

To help the England team prepare for Portugal the Football Association invited Japan and Iceland to compete in a triangular mini-tournament at the City of Manchester City Stadium.

Traditionally not a lot should be read into such games. They are only friendly internationals and the main purpose of the exercise is to fine tune tactics, improve match fitness and give everyone in the squad a final run-out before the real business begins.

But as fans we don't always see it that way...

England 1 v 1 Japan

The first England international to be staged at the impressive City of Manchester Stadium proved to be a huge anti-climax.

With, what almost everyone agreed was, our best eleven, failure to beat Japan was a bitter disappointment.

As expected, Sven opted for the diamond formation in midfield and while not many will argue with his selection of Frank Lampard in the side, the decision to play him in the holding midfield role was slightly baffling.

Despite some neat touches and impressive interplay from Lamps it didn't really work and he'd be much more effective in an advanced midfield position.

Michael Owen's 25th international goal, a typical poachers effort, was a good sign and should have been the signal for the floodgates to open but it just didn't materialise.

Alarmingly Japan were allowed far too much time and space, and it came as no surprise when they deservedly drew level eight minutes after the break through Shinji Ono.

Owen and Beckham went close to restoring England's lead afterwards but it required a late save from David James to spare our blushes and save us from an embarrassing defeat against a nation who are hardly regarded as one of football's superpowers.

In the end a draw was probably a fair result but not one that bodes well for Euro 2004, which is suddenly drawing ever closer.

Too many players were off colour today and with just one warm-up game left Sven has some work to do if he is to reassure us that we're not just going out there to make up the numbers.

Team: James, Gary Neville (P Neville, 86), Terry (King, 88), Campbell, Ashley Cole; Lampard (Butt, 81), Beckham (Joe Cole, 77), Gerrard (Hargreaves, 81), Scholes (Dyer, 77); Owen (Vassell, 77), Rooney (Heskey, 77)

England 6 v 1 Iceland

This was more like it and we head off to Portugal in better spirits after Iceland were emphatically hit for six.

Following the unconvincing draw with Japan it was with a mixture of relief and happiness to see normal service resumed

The performance was in complete contrast to the events of four days previous and a huge confidence booster ahead of our eagerly anticipated opening Euro 2004 clash with France in just over a week's time.

The boys responded to the carnival atmosphere inside the City of Manchester Stadium by doing what they should have done to Japan. The diamond formation was ditched in favour of the more traditional 4-4-2 and the only changes in personnel saw Jamie Carragher come in for the injured John Terry and Paul Robinson replace David James in goal.

Both performed commendably, to prove that they are more than able deputies, and their sound displays were mirrored by the rest of the team, in what was a very one-sided affair.

Once Frank Lampard opened the scoring with a deflected shot after 24 minutes there was no way back into the game for the hapless Icelanders and any fear that England would sit back on their lead, as they did against Japan, were dispelled two minutes later when Rooney finished off a superb cross by Gary Neville.

Shortly before the interval the Everton teenager doubled his tally with a sublime long-range

effort to prove once and for all that he's ready to be unleashed on the big stage in Portugal.

The visitors managed to pull a goal back on the stroke of half-time by exposing some sloppiness in the England defence but as a contest this game was already over and Sven made nine changes during the interval.

One of the fresh faces was Darius Vassell and he continued his impressive scoring form at international level by bagging a brace of goals as the strength in depth of our squad shone through.

In between the Villa striker netting Wayne Bridge got on the scoresheet for his country for the first time and it was just a pity Paul Scholes wasn't still on the pitch because he won't have a better chance of ending his now much-publicised England drought.

Overall this was a highly satisfactory way to wrap up our preparations and buzz that was missing in the aftermath of the draw with Japan has most certainly returned.

The start of Euro 2004 cannot come around quick enough now. Bring on the French!

Team: Robinson (Walker): G Neville (P Neville 45), Campbell (King 45), Carragher (Defoe 84), A Cole (Bridge 45); Beckham (Hargreaves 45), Lampard (Butt 45), Gerrard (Dyer 45), Scholes (J Cole 45); Owen (Vassell 45), Rooney (Heskey 45)

THE FINALS ARRIVE

JUNE 12TH

After all the hype the big day finally arrives. Euro 2004 kicks off in Oporto and the host nation crash to a shock 2-1 defeat against Greece. What a way to start the tournament.

It was a result that sent shockwaves reverberating around the whole of Europe, never mind Portugal, and the locals are understandably in mourning after watching their heroes suffer stage fright on the opening night.

To compound their misery, Iberian rivals Spain later confirmed their credentials as one of the pre-tournament favourites with a 1-0 victory over Russia in Faro-Loule.

With the finals up and running the majority of England's barmy army are packed into the sun-drenched bars of the Algarve and all the talk is of tomorrow's big game against France.

Ahead of the mass exodus to Lisbon the mood is one of optimism and you can feel the sense of excitement steadily building.

In the capital, supporters are now arriving in their droves. The welcome, like the weather, has been a warm one and even a minor disturbance in the main square failed to dampen the friendly atmosphere.

The major talking point centres around who should replace John Terry at the heart of the England defence against the French.

It was confirmed yesterday that Terry has failed to prove his fitness and the breaking news today is that Ledley King is likely to be given the nod over Jamie Carragher to replace him.

There's no doubt the loss of Terry is a big blow to our chances of kicking off the tournament with a moral-boosting victory over the reigning champions and, we're not going to pretend otherwise, but it's time to put our faith in young Ledley.

There has been a lot of support among the fans for Sven to go with Carragher, especially given his greater experience on the big stage.

His track record against Thierry Henry, however, is not good. He's been given the run around by the Arsenal star too many times in Liverpool colours and for this reason King is probably the safer bet.

It'll be by far the biggest game the Tottenham player has ever played and fingers crossed he will rise to the occasion. The prospect of facing Thierry Henry will probably mean he won't get much sleep tonight

Good news from the French camp is that Marcel Desailly will start on the bench.

France are the favourites and the task facing us is a daunting one but let's remember we are England and on our day we are capable of mixing it with the best of them.

A draw would probably be a good result to open with but it would be nice to put one over our friends from across the Channel and there's no doubt every English man and woman would settle for a scrappy 1-0 win.

THE FINALS ARRIVE

JUNE 13TH

> "A warm Sunday evening, 35,000 euphoric fans all eagerly awaiting England v France! No I wasn't in Portugal, I was at the Isle of Wight rock festival! Of course for the majority of the 35,000 strong crowd the main event was David Bowie but never the less the atmosphere was electric and all involved, male/female, young/old, football lovers/haters were singing the old England Classics." - Ian Chiverton

> "Everywhere you go you see flags on cars, on houses and all over the pubs. You just know there must be a big game coming. The day of the France v England game is here, cars would beep at others who show their allegiance to our boys. We're confident of victory, the TV tells us the Manager and the team are confident of victory. There's a small appetiser before the game with the Swiss playing Croatia, even though you try and concentrate on that game you know what's coming, and you know that as with all-important England games your going to be taken for a ride. England don't always deliver but boy you know there will be headlines made and hero's created." - Andy Smith

England 1 v 2 France

Gutted, devastated, shocked and stunned are the words that best sum up the mood of every English man and woman after witnessing this cruellest of defeats.

Frank Lampard's first half header had set us up for a famous victory. The 90 minutes were up and injury time was slowly ticking by. The reigning European champions' long unbeaten run was about to end and our Euro 2004 campaign was seemingly off to a flier. The champagne was on ice and an entire nation was ready to party.

Then came a needless foul by substitute Emile Heskey. A free-kick was awarded in a dangerous position and up stepped that French midfield maestro Zinedine Zidane. In a flash the score was level. David James was left rooted to the spot and could only watch in despair as ZZ's perfectly executed set-piece nestled into the back of his net.

The thought of having to settle for a draw at this stage was a bitter pill to swallow but on reflection we'd have gladly settled for that because it was about to get worse.

Moments later, for reasons only he will know, Steven Gerrard played a careless back-pass that fell short of its intended target.

The jet-heeled Thierry Henry chased after it. David James rushed off his line in a desperate attempt to get there first. Unfortunately he didn't. Henry's legs were taken from him, a penalty was awarded and our world was about to collapse.

An eerie nervous tension hung over the stadium as the ice-cool Zidane boldly placed the ball on the spot. We held our collective breath and prayed that he'd miss but with the clinical assurance you'd expect from one of the planet's greatest players he sent James the wrong way to confirm our worst fears.

An overwhelming sense of disbelief engulfed us and tears were unashamedly shed. The subdued atmosphere was in stark contrast to the one that had greeted the arrival of the teams two hours earlier.

England fans had impressively taken over the Estadio da Luz in Lisbon. The Mackem contingent among us may think their Stadium

of Light is impressive but it's nothing compared to the Portuguese version,

The neutrals in the crowd could've been forgiven for thinking they were at the new Wembley. The hairs on the back of our necks stood to attention as one of the most rousing renditions of 'God Save the Queen' bellowed around this breathtaking bowl and the French, as experienced as they are on the big stage, must have been intimidated.

But if they were it didn't show once the first whistle sounded. It was they who started brightest. Trezeguet headed narrowly over and Makelele shot wide. England took time to find their feet and it was a totally unexpected lead we took, six minutes before the break.

Beckham was fouled by Lizarazu on the right edge of the penalty area and the resultant free-kick was delivered with pin-point accuracy onto the head of Lampard who directed the ball into Fabien Barthez's top left hand corner.

For one tiny moment time seemed to stand still, as the shock of seeing that ball hit the back of the net sank in. Then sheer pandemonium took over and England fans erupted in joyous celebration. We won't deny Lampard's goal came against the run of play but who cared?

The half-time break came and went, and as you'd expect it was France who were enjoying the greater share of possession as they strove to get back into the game. The odd pot-shot at James apart though, we never really felt threatened and in the 72nd minute a famous victory should have been wrapped up.

Teenage striking sensation Wayne Rooney burst through the opposition defence only to be hacked down in the box by Silvestre.

There was no question about whether or not it was a penalty and the Man United defender was lucky to only be shown a yellow card for his misdemeanour.

With an entire nation willing him on our captain stepped up to take the kick. Memories of his woeful effort from 12-yards out in Istanbul momentarily flashed through our minds as he placed the ball on the spot but surely lightening couldn't strike twice.

We prayed it wouldn't. But sadly it did. Beckham's former Old Trafford team-mate Barthez guessed correctly and dived to his right to pull off a fine save.

We then hoped it wouldn't matter. The closing stages of the game were almost upon us. France were hardly laying siege to our goal and what they had thrown at us had been dealt with comfortably.

As the minutes ticked by and the score remained 1-0 an historic victory was within our grasp. The least said about what happened next the better.

Seeing Zidane's two goals hit the back of our net was like being hit twice in quick succession by a sledgehammer and they'll no doubt haunt us many years to come.

Now we know how the Bayern Munich fans felt at the end of that never-to-be-forgotten European Cup Final of 1999. But we live to fight another day. Failure to win the opening game in a tournament is not the end of the world and the overall performance of the boys was one that left us with genuine grounds for optimism.

Player Ratings

David James - 6

His critics will argue he should have at least made an attempt to stop the free-kick but he can't be faulted for conceding the penalty and the final few minutes apart had little else to do.

Garry Neville - 7

As you'd expect, kept his cool in the heat of the battle and did what was required of him. Was forced onto his back-foot a little too often for his liking but stayed calm and composed throughout.

Ashley Cole - 7

Impressively quelled the threat posed by his Highbury team-mate Pires and caught the eye with some impressive attacking forays into opposition territory.

Ledley King - 8

An outstanding performance from the youngster. Didn't put a foot wrong and fully justified Sven's faith in him. Now has a genuine case for a regular starting place.

Sol Campbell - 8

An awesome display from the big man. Had Trezeguet in his pocket all night and was dominant figure at the heart of our defence. Didn't deserve to be on the losing side.

Steven Gerrard - 5

Failed to live up to expectations. Was relatively quiet and his uncharacteristic bad mistake at the end capped an overall disappointing performance.

Frank Lampard - 8

Our most impressive midfield performer. Took his goal well and must surely have established himself as a first choice member of Sven's starting eleven now.

Paul Scholes - 6

Still struggling to rediscover his true form and made little impact from his position out on the left of midfield.

David Beckham - 7

Great delivery to Lampard for the opening goal but his missed penalty proved costly. To be fair, Barthez has to be given credit for the save but Becks should have scored and he knows it.

Micheal Owen - 5

An ineffective display from our supposed most lethal striker but what do you expect when he's starved of service? Hardly had a sniff at goal all match and it was no surprise he came off.

Wayne Rooney - 8

Frightened the life out of the experienced French defence with an exceptional performance that belied his tender years. Deserved a goal when brought down for the penalty and had he stayed on may well have got one.

Substitutes

Darius Vassell (on for Owen) - 6

Livened up the attack by running at the French.

Emile Heskey (on for Rooney) - 5

Gave away the foul that led to France's equaliser.

Owen Hargreaves (on for Scholes) - 5

Failed to create much of an impression.

"We'd lost in the worst, most shocking possible fashion yet all these music lovers still had as much faith in there team as at half past 9. These music lovers showed the beauty of a competition like this, the way it brings all genres and generations together even if just for a month, its fans like these that should spur the likes of Beckham and co on to success." - Iain Chiverton

"The day we've been waiting for - the chance for my son and I to watch England in a big tournament against one of the best teams in the world, in the way that I watched England v Brazil with my dad in 1970. We've collected the medals, we've analysed the squad, he's copied the haircuts but now it's about football and the joys of passing on England supportership to the next generation.

"We shout, we cheer, we watch every move and count every second. We dance with joy at Beckham and Lampard's double act. We swear we would never have played anyone but Ledley King in defence. We love the Arsenal players who we would normally hate in the Premiership because this is England and we're winning 1-0. We cover our eyes and peep out to watch the missed penalty. We tell ourselves it's nearly all over but one of us knows it's never over until the whistle and here it is. The free kick, Zidane, the goal, 2 points lost. The back-pass from Gerrard, the foul from James and the penalty.

"Welcome to being an England supporter my son. It's a hard path to follow but this family have been doing it for generations." - Kim Dewdney

"A meeting with supposedly the best team in the world had ended with defeat, at a time when the whole nation was confident we could beat them. With stars such as David Beckham, Michael Owen, Steven Gerrard and Wayne Rooney you come to expect great things of this England team, yet we fell short again. The fact is only one of those players mentioned lived up to expectations on a night where all of them needed to shine." - Dominic Jackson

"After watching the England v France game on television, I thought that a combination of errors were to blame for the two Zidane injury-time goals. First of all Heskey gave a silly foul away on the edge of the penalty area. Then as the wall was being arranged, Ashley Cole should have stood on the line because how many times have we all seen him clear off the line for Arsenal during the season just gone? Then the penalty, what can I say it was a stupid back pass from Gerrard and I thought James made the right choice to bring Henry down, otherwise you'd put your house on him to score. At least he still had the chance to save the penalty. I think England can do well from this, they played really well, a shame we lost but I still think we have a great chance this year. ROOOOOOOOONNNEEEEEYYYYYY!!!!!!!" - Alex Walke

JUNE 14TH

As the dramatic events of last night start to sink in, David Beckham has held his hands up and says he's to blame for our agonising loss against France.

True, his second half penalty miss was a costly error and respect to him for his honesty. But it would be too easy to point the finger solely at the skipper for not converting from 12-yards out.

Emile Heskey and Steven Gerrard were guilty of mistakes that helped the French snatch victory from the jaws of defeat. Sven's tactics have also come under scrutiny and we could go on forever analysing where we went wrong but so long as the aforementioned individuals learn from their mistakes what is the point?

What's done is done and, as painful as it was, looking for a scapegoat is not going to change the result now. Instead, it's time for everyone to pull together, get behind the team and concentrate on the forthcoming games against Switzerland and Croatia because they are what are most important now.

Thankfully the mood of utter despondency didn't lead to the outbreaks of violence that the Portuguese police may have been expecting. We shook hands with the French supporters at the end and, through gritted teeth, congratulated them on their victory, before drowning our sorrows in the bars of Lisbon.

Sadly the same cannot be said of the fans back home in blighty, who after a night on the ale in

Chapter Six THE FINALS ARRIVE

their local, found defeat too hard to take. After the roller-coaster of emotions we went through last night it's a relief to step out of the spotlight today and it was nice to sit back, relax and watch another set of fans go through it all on the television.

The much-fancied Italians are up first. They fail to impress against Denmark and are lucky to escape with a goalless draw but the Swedes, inspired by the returning Henrik Larsson sent out a warning to the other competing nations by romping to an emphatic 5-0 success over Bulgaria

"It's the morning after the night before. It didn't really happen, did it? We did not deserve to lose that game. The harsh reality is that we did. But lets face it, we didn't deserve to win it either. A draw though? Surely.

"We've gone and battled our hearts out against arguably the best side in the world and been cruelly beaten. I've had a day and a half to digest it now and I honestly believe it's the best thing that could have happened to us. We've got a squad out there packed full of very talented and very proud young men. These same young men now have the incentive and the belief to truly believe that they can go all the way. Sure, they said it before... but did they really believe it? I don't think so.

"For 90 minutes they went toe to toe with Henry, Zizou and company and were within a whisker of winning the game. We defended resolutely throughout without ever offering too much going forward. We didn't threaten them enough. We didn't impose our game on them. Our drive and our desire, though clearly evident seemed almost stifled (Rooney apart, an 18 year old epitomising everything we should be about) by the fear and respect we bestowed on our opposition. The noises coming out of the camp now are defiant. They want another pop at these French guys. They KNOW they can beat them. And I reckon that if they want it badly enough they've got every chance. We're right behind you... COME ON ENGLAND!!!" - Keith Jones

THE FINALS ARRIVE

JUNE 15TH

England may not be in action last night but unfortunately that doesn't stop trouble erupting in Albufeira, where English holiday makers clash with the local police. With UEFA threatening to kick Sven's men out of the tournament should such scenes have been repeated this is behaviour we could well do without.

Not surprisingly, the events in the Algarve make the headline news this morning. Thankfully, the vast travelling contingent of England fans have behaved exemplary.

Genuine fans don't condone what went on but as a UEFA spokesman has come out and said it is unrelated to the football so why should the team be punished? Lets just hope the good behaviour that goes unreported continues and that the action on the pitch is not overshadowed by further outbreaks of violence off it.

Back to the football and Latvia, the expected whipping boys in the so-called group of death, surprise us all by actually scoring a goal and then almost pull of a shock victory over the much-fancied Czech Republic.

It requires two late goals to spare Czech blushes and the Liverpool fans among us were pleased to see Milan Baros on the scoresheet. We know how the Latvians must feel and have every sympathy with them.

The big game of the day takes place later in the evening between Holland and Germany. The sparks usually fly when these two bitter rivals clash but a rather tame 1-1 draw helps lift the spirits of the watching England fans who admit they wouldn't mind facing either side later in the tournament on the evidence of this showing.

The most impressive sight of the night is the thousands of orange-clad Dutch fans who brighten up the Estadio da Dragoa.

As per normal they are here to back their team in large numbers but not of the size to rival the phenomenal contingent that is in Portugal to back England.

JUNE 16TH

As the dust finally begins to settle on our dramatic defeat against France and the post-match inquests are wound up the focus turns to tomorrow's clash with the Swiss in Coimbra.

It's a must win game and the pressure is on. On paper we should win. Switzerland didn't exactly set the tournament alight in their opening game against Croatia but you can feel a slight nervous tension among the fans ahead of the game.

That nervousness is probably not helped by stories in the press today in which David James revealed he was not shown any videos of Zidane taking free-kicks ahead of the French match.

Chapter Six THE FINALS ARRIVE

It's not the first time old Jamo has tried to cover up his goalkeeping deficiencies with a bizarre excuse and let's just be thankful he hasn't brought his Playstation with him! Another major story emanating today concerns Steven Gerrard and a possible £50 million transfer from Liverpool to Chelsea. Nothing to do with England you'd think but it could have an adverse effect.

Just because Russia are out of the tournament Roman Abramovich is doing his best to hamper England's prospects by trying to unsettle one of our star players. Hopefully, Stevie will take no notice of the speculation and remain focussed on the task in hand, but if someone was dangling such a lucrative carrot in front of you be honest and try telling yourself you wouldn't think about it!

On the injury front Paul Scholes is reported to be a doubt after twisting his ankle on Sunday. Normally this would be considered a catastrophic blow but so poor has Scholesy's form been of late, the majority of supporters heading north to Coimbra are openly discussing that is could well be a blessing in disguise. One player who definitely won't be involved is Scholes' Manchester United team-mate Nicky

Butt, who has failed to recover from a knee injury and will probably play no part in the tournament whatsoever. The fact that he probably wouldn't have played anyway means this is no big loss either.

Following his admission yesterday that his penalty miss cost England victory against France, Becks now insists he will continue taking the spot kicks. Fair play to him for his bravery but surely it's about time he handed over the responsibility.

Elsewhere today, the hosts are back in action and know they must get something out of their game with Russia if they are to avoid the embarrassment of an early exit. The situation they find themselves in is pretty similar to ours and with the pressure on they manage to pull it out of the bag and claim a slender victory over the disappointing Russians who deservedly, and not surprisingly, are now out of the tournament.

The Greeks continue to shock and despite going a goal down to Spain they hit back to force a draw and virtually book their place in the last eight, which is amazing when you consider they were 100/1 outsiders before the start of the tournament.

JUNE 17TH

"Let's stop all the crying about the France game, that's in the past. Come on boys roll all over the Swiss!"

- Jenny Groves

"Why is Sven persisting with Scholes? His recent form does not warrant a place in the starting eleven. Reputation alone is keeping him in the team. Surely Kieron Dyer would be a better bet down the left against a side like Switzerland." - Gary Moorcroft

"Lose this and we might as well pack up and come home. Gerrard, Beckham, Owen and Scholes it's time you pulled your fingers out. To do well in a major tournament your big players have to perform. This is an ideal opportunity. Let's do it and do it in style." - Martin Mitchell

England 3 v 0 Switzerland

A new epidemic is threatening to engulf Euro 2004. It's called Rooney-mania and opposition defences were left frantically searching for a cure after watching Everton's teenage striking sensation inspire England to a comfortable 3-0 victory over Switzerland.

After the heartbreaking loss against the French this was just what the doctor ordered and our hopes of progressing from the opening group phase look a whole lot healthier now. As expected, John Terry took his place in the starting eleven after recovering from injury. Ledley King could count himself very unlucky to be the player forced to make way but given the Chelsea's man's greater experience it's a decision that doesn't cause too many ripples of discontent among the fans.

The English invasion of the normally sedate university city of Coimbra had begun 24 hours earlier. The peace and tranquillity that the Portuguese students are normally accustomed to has been shattered but the banter with the locals is all good natured.

Before kick-off the Swiss made an amusing attempt to taunt us by unfurling a banner that read 'Go home – try cricket'. Full marks to them for their effort but just over 90 minutes later it was they who were on the receiving end as chants of 'Are You Scotland In Disguise' rang in their ears as they sheepishly slipped out of the stadium.

England began the game tentatively but early Swiss pressure was soaked up with ease and after 24 minutes the deadlock was broken. In what was our first meaningful attack Gerrard and Beckham atoned for their errors against France by combining delightfully down the right flank. Owen's cross found Rooney and he directed his header past the keeper from close-range.

In opening the scoring, Rooney created history by becoming the youngest-ever goalscorer in the European Championships but it was with our hearts in our mouths that we then watched him celebrate with a circus-style somersault.

He has suddenly emerged as England's most important player and we could've done without seeing him risk injury in such a way, although there was never much chance of that. This boy can seemingly do everything and if the gymnastic judges were present they'd have probably gave him a 10 out of 10 for that as well.

The goal was another that had come against the run of play but also one that helped settle our early nerves. How we'd have coped had Frei not spurned a glorious opportunity to equalise moments later we'll never know but thankfully it was the last decent chance Switzerland were to create.

In relation to France, the Swiss were pretty poor and it didn't take much for us to finish them off. Without having to move into the high gears England gradually stamped their authority on the proceedings and following the dismissal of West Brom full-back Bernt Haas on the hour mark there was only ever going to be one outcome.

With 15 minutes to go another chapter was added to the ever-increasing Rooney legend when the 18-year old Scouser doubled his and England's advantage with a clinically taken strike from the edge of the box that came back off the post before hitting the keeper on the head and crossing the line.

With the painful memories of Zidane still too fresh in the mind this second 'killer' goal came as a huge relief and, with the pressure off, England began to play their best football of the match.

A highly satisfactory afternoon was rounded off when Gerrard notched a third and final goal minutes from time. Neville and Beckham rolled back the years to set up Gerrard and the Liverpool skipper side-footed neatly into the roof of the net to complete the scoring.

Substitutes Hargreaves and Vassell had chances to extend the lead even further in the closing stages but any more than three would have been harsh on the Swiss and would have flattered us to be honest. This wasn't a spectacular performance by any means but with Rooney in such hot form a place in the last eight should be ours and the signs are there that this team can get better as the tournaments moves on.

Player Ratings

David James - 6
Did not look too convincing when put under pressure but kept a clean sheet and didn't really have much to do in terms of making saves.

Garry Neville - 7
Defensively sound and got forward well. The Swiss could find no way past him when they attacked down the left, while at the opposite end he had a telling role to play in our final goal.

Ashley Cole - 7
Offensively caught the eye again with the way he exploited large gaps down the opposition right and coped easily with what eve was thrown at him defensively.

Sol Campbell - 8
Unflappable yet again, big Sol lived up to his rock-like reputation with another dominant performance. Kept the Swiss at bay with ease and never looked troubled.

John Terry - 6
A stuttering return to the side for Terry, who looked nervous and took time to settle. Can play better and he'll have to if he wants to keep his place ahead of King.

Steven Gerrard - 8
A much-improved performance by Stevie G. His strong forward running helped England dominate and a well-taken goal capped a satisfactory afternoon's work.

Frank Lampard - 8
Another faultless display from a player who seems to be getting better and better. Passed the ball well and worked hard for the duration.

David Beckham - 7
Failed to get a firm grip of the game like you'd expect from an England skipper but made a telling contribution to two of the goals and was dangerous from every set-piece.

Paul Scholes - 5
Scholesy's form is becoming more and more of a worry. Looked decidedly off-colour again and offered little to the victory. Seems to be suffering from a lack of confidence and desperately needs a goal.

Wayne Rooney - 9
Simply sensational. England's worst kept secret is now well and truly out of the bag. On the evidence of this showing Rooney can fire us to glory.

Michael Owen - 6
Struggled once again to make an impact and does not look the player he once was. Did well to set up Rooney's opening goal but overall he looked tired and out-of-sorts.

Substitutes

Owen Hargreaves (on for Scholes) - 6
Came on for the last 20 minutes and did well.

Darius Vassell (on for Owen) - 6
Used his pace to good effect and was unlucky not to get on the scoresheet.

Kieron Dyer (on for Rooney) - 7
Showed brief glimpses of his skill but was only on for seven minutes.

THE FINALS ARRIVE

JUNE 18TH

Sven denies a player revolt forced him to ditch the diamond formation but to put it bluntly, who cares what forced him to change his tactics? It worked and that's all we care about. Whoever's decision it was – thanks very much. And let's make sure we keep playing this way in future games.

As we bask in the glory of last night's success UEFA have quite rightly confirmed that England's second goal against the Swiss will be awarded to Wayne Rooney.

There were fears that it would go down as an own goal by the keeper but there's no doubt Rooney deserves the goal and for once the UEFA bigwigs have made a sensible decision.

Croatia's surprise 2-2 draw with France in Leiria last night, coupled with our win over the Swiss, means just a point is required from our final group game to ensure qualification. Top spot is also still a possibility so there's everything to play for against Croatia on Monday.

In what was the game of the tournament so far today, Sweden score a late goal to force a 1-1 draw with Italy. The Italian's are traditionally slow starters to major competitions but this was their second successive draw and they now face the real prospect of going home early.

One team that will be on the first plane home is Bulgaria, whose hopes are dead and buried after their uneventful 2-0 loss to Denmark.

JUNE 19TH

The Germans have an Englishman to thank for not being on the receiving end of major shock result this afternoon.

Everyone's favourite Premiership referee Mike Riley failed to award the minnows of Latvia a cast-iron penalty in their Group D encounter with Germany and his ill-judged decision enables Rudi Voeller's team to escape with a goalless draw in a match they were expected to stroll through.

Still it's nice to see the Germans struggling, but it could have been much worse for them had it not been for Herr Riley!

It's the first time the Rotherham-born official

has officiated at a big international tournament and he's done his prospects of being invited back no favours with this performance.

In the same group, Czech Republic, the pre-tournament dark horses, show their class by recovering from a two goals down to clinch a thrilling 3-2 victory over the Dutch in Aviero.

It was a game that had everything and was easily the best of the tournament so far. Like France v Portugal in '84 and England v Holland in '96 it will be remembered as one of the European Championship's all-time classics and no doubt replayed many times in future years.

The Czech's look to be in phenomenal form and

on the evidence of this latest showing there's no doubt that they're the team to avoid when the knockout stage gets underway.

Not that we should be thinking of the latter rounds just yet. There's a job to be done against Croatia first of all and their coach says he is determined to celebrate his 72nd birthday by qualifying for the quarter-final at our expense. All the best for today Otto, but don't expect England to be bearing any gifts in Lisbon on Monday!

JUNE 20TH

The English public just can't get enough of Wayne Rooney and every word that is printed about him in the newspapers makes for compulsive reading.

Today he's featured in the press saying he won't curb his temper, despite pleas from some of the senior members in the squad who fear he could become a victim of over zealous referees.

Aggression is a major part of Rooney's game and helps make him such the special player he is. Our advice to Wayne would be keep playing your normal game. You're doing great and we're right behind you.

One team who have escaped being given the Rooney run around are Spain.

The Spaniards were up to their old tricks once again today and exited a major tournament at the first hurdle after failing to get the necessary point in the eagerly anticipated 'Iberian derby' clash with hosts Portugal.

In a match that failed to live up to its pre-match hype the Portuguese deservedly came out on top to take their place in the last eight and send the Spanish home. Nuno Gomes' goal is the cue for a carnival on the streets of Lisbon and as we converge on the capital in readiness for our own crunch clash against Croatia tomorrow we look on and hope that in 24 hours time we'll be involved in similar scenes of joy.

Down in Faro-Loule, Greece, the surprise package of the tournament so far, secure their place in the last eight despite losing to Russia in their final group game.

Even the most diehard Greek supporter will not have expected their team to have come this far and surely it must be free the kebab's all round tonight!

Hopefully, England will join them in the quarter-final.

Our big game with the Croats is now less than 24 hours away and there is an air of quiet confidence among the fans who are watching tonight's action on the giant screens in Lisbon's main city centre square's.

Same again please Sven!

JUNE 21ST

"We arrived early in Lisbon for the vital match against Croatia and you could already feel the atmosphere. It was like a carnival. Rossio Square in the city centre was decked out in St George flags with names of different towns on them. What a superb spectacle this was. It made you so proud to be English and for the team to have such a massive following was superb.

"After we had managed to find a place to hang a flag up we then went straight to the bar got the beers out and headed over to where the England Supporters band was. We then started to have a singsong with around 10,000 other fans. It was just awesome and it carried on for a few hours until we decided to head towards the stadium." - Ian O'Neill

England 4 v 2 Croatia

Is there anything this boy cannot do?

Wayne Rooney just gets better and better. So much so that we're running out of superlatives to describe him.

Not content with his two-goal super show against the Swiss, the most exciting young talent at Euro 2004 repeats the feat against Croatia and sends England triumphantly into the last eight of the tournament. Tonight proves, once and for all, that Rooney really has now come of age on the international stage. And to complete a memorable night, Paul Scholes ended his much-publicised England goal famine.

After our brief sojourn in Coimbra it was back to the modern day Portuguese capital and to our adopted home ground the Stadium of Light for this crunch clash with the Croats.

9,000 opposition fans contributed to another electric atmosphere but they were easily drowned out by an impressive army of England support that seems to be getting bigger and bigger with each game.

Looking resplendent in red, Sven's men took to the pitch amid a cacophony of noise and, as we've come to expect now, the national anthem was sung with commendable gusto.

Everything was set up perfectly but within minutes of the first whistle Becks carelessly gave a free-kick away on our right and from the resultant free-kick Croatia stunned us all by snatching the lead.

Ashley Cole, under pressure from a Croatian striker, made a rare mistake and could only knock the ball back towards James when he should have cleared. The keeper did well to parry the ball away but John Terry hesitated and the ball fell invitingly to the feet of Nico Kovac, who made no mistake from close-range.

The majority of the ground fell silent. The game was still in its infancy but our best-laid plans were in danger of going up in smoke. Croatia had aspirations of a place in the last eight themselves. Only a win would suffice for them and with their noses in front it was going to be difficult to peg them back.

But the shock of conceding that early goal stung us into action and soon we were playing some delightful football.

An equalising goal just had to come.

Suddenly we were well on top and when our breakthrough came it was fully deserved. A few chances had earlier gone begging and in the back of our mind was that nagging doubt that maybe this wasn't going to be our night. Until Scholesy finally delivered that is.

The United man's nightmare in front of goal looked like it was going to continue when he wasted a golden opportunity to level the scores shortly after the opening goal. With only the keeper to beat he shot straight at him but his time was to finally come in the 40th minute.

Rooney flicked the ball into his path and Scholes ghosted through to head beyond the Croatia keeper and end his 31-game barren run. The look of relief and delight on his face was palpable. A huge weight had been lifted from his shoulders and suddenly Manchester's most famous ginger was back to his old self.

Within five minutes he returned the compliment and teed up Rooney for a breathtaking strike that almost burst the net. With the half-time break upon us it was a crucial time to score and our passage to the quarter-final looked a safe bet.

England's confidence was understandably sky-high as they strolled out for the second half. And it showed. Owen and Scholes went close to increasing the lead and the Croats were there for the taking.

It was no surprise when 2-1 became 3-1. Rooney was again the goalscorer and although he will score more spectacular goals this was a typical striker's effort.

The Everton youngster played a beautiful one-two with Owen, then raced through on goal with just the keeper to beat. The ease in which he subsequently tucked the ball home was amazing for a player so young and a pleasure to see.

England were cruising but some slack defending allowed Igor Tudor to pull a goal back and the nightmare scenario of a Croatian comeback had us all slightly worried until Frank Lampard restored out two-goal advantage two minutes later.

Lampard's sweet left-footed finish capped another fine display by the ever-improving Chelsea midfielder but understandably the post-match plaudits were reserved for one man only.

The whole of Europe now know what Evertonian's have long known. Wayne Rooney is one of the most precocious talents in the game and the fact we have him in our ranks makes us the envy of every other nation in Euro 2004.

There is now a genuine belief that we could go all the way and, with the boy Rooney in such inspired form, no defence in the tournament will relish the prospect of having to shackle him in the knockout stages

Player Ratings

David James - 8
His best game of the tournament yet. Made some vital saves to keep the Croats at bay during a crucial time in the match and was helpless to prevent the two opposition goals.

Gary Neville - 8
Accomplished as ever and a shining light throughout the 90 minutes. It's hard to pick a fault in Neville's game at the moment and long may it continue.

Ashley Cole - 6
Was at fault for Croatia's opening goal but to his credit he didn't let it affect his game.

Quickly regained his composure and made amends for his early error.

Sol Campbell - 8
Another polished performance by a player who must now rank as one of the best defenders in Europe. A reassuring presence at the back who seems to thrive in the big-match atmosphere.

John Terry - 7
Was slow to react when Croatia took their early lead but hardly put a foot wrong for the remainder of the night and looked much more fitter and confident than in the game against the Swiss.

Steven Gerrard - 7
A tireless performance from the Liverpool captain but there still seems to something missing from his game and his tendency to attempt the spectacular when something more simple would do is becoming a source of irritation.

Frank Lampard - 8
Calm and composed in the centre of the park, he ran the show for the 84 minutes he was on the pitch and his goal was the icing on the cake for him.

David Beckham - 7
Still not at his best but worked hard and played an influential captain's role. Hopefully, we'll see the real Becks in the knockout phase.

Paul Scholes - 8
Back among the goals after an incredible 2,257-minute famine on the international stage and, on the evidence of his overall performance, seemingly back to his best.

Wayne Rooney - 10
An unbelievable performance from someone so young. No other words can describe his performance and had he not been taken off he'd have no doubt walked away with the match ball. Wrap him up in cotton wool until the quarter-final, please!

Michael Owen - 7
A much-improved performance from the original boy wonder. The master is showing signs of developing a potentially lethal strike partnership with his apprentice and that can only augur well for the knockout stage.

Substitutes

Ledley King (on for Scholes) - 5
Didn't put a foot wrong in the twenty minutes he was on.

Darius Vassell (on for Rooney) - 5
Was constantly on the lookout for a goal.

Phil Neville (on for Lampard) - 5
Slotted in well for the remaining six minutes.

"I had the good fortune to win a two day trip for the England v Croatia game from the Daily Record. Yes, I am Scottish. But I had a great time. During the trip to Lisbon I did not see one bit of trouble and I found myself rooting for England during the game. The one thing that will live in my memory is seeing Wayne Rooney in the flesh. What strength and ability this boy has. I only hope that the hype does not destroy him."

John McKenzie

"How an earth will Everton be able to keep hold of Rooney now? This boy deserves to be plying his trade on the big stage week in, week out. No disrespect to the Toffeemen but he's wasted at Goodison." - Terry Ogilvy

"It looks as though we're hitting form at just the right time. We've been fairly lucky with injuries so far in the tournament and fingers crossed it continues. If we can keep a settled side for the next three games, I honestly cannot see anyone stopping us. Cue Baddiel and Skinner; 'It's coming home, it's coming . . .'"

- Drew Checkland

JUNE 22ND

It's with a thumping head and beaming smile that many English men and women awake this morning.

Johan Vonlanthen, in Switzerland's defeat to France last night, may have stolen Wayne Rooney's record as the youngest goalscorer in the history of the European Championship's but the tournament's man-of-the-moment deservedly adorns the front page of almost every newspaper this morning.

His fame has now reached such a level that comparisons are being made between him and the most revered figure in football history Pele.

Such comparisons are often misjudged and unfair but it's a measure of Rooney's remarkable progress that there's hardly any pundits queuing up to disagree with such a sentiment.

Chants of 'Rooo-ney! Rooo-ney!' are still ringing in our ears and there's a spring in our step, the kind of which we've not experienced since Euro '96.

We're three games from glory and with many of the fancied sides on their way home from

Portugal the Henri Delauney trophy is there for the taking.

France's 4-2 victory over Switzerland means we finish second in our group and must play host nation Portugal in the quarter-final.

Obviously, we'd have preferred to play the Greeks but it wasn't to be and, to be honest, the mood of every England fan at the moment is that we fear no-one. Our main worry now is getting our hands on tickets for the Portugal game.

The latest big name to bow out of the tournament is Italy. A last-minute goal ensures the Azzurri complete their group matches with a win over Bulgaria but a controversial 2-2 draw between Scandinavian neighbours Denmark and Sweden means they go out on goal difference.

Any result other than a 2-2 draw in the Nordic derby would have been enough to ensure Italy of qualification and the noises coming out of their camp afterwards suggests they smell a rat.

To be fair, there was nothing to suggest that

the Swedes and Danes manufactured their result and UEFA are, quite rightly, quick to play down such talk.

On a sad note football was put into perspective today when news broke that an England fan who had been stabbed last night, lost his fight for life in a Portuguese hospital.

Stephen Smith, 28, of Wolverhampton was an innocent victim of an attempted robbery just hours after the game against Croatia.

The England team will wear black armbands in memory of him against Portugal and our deepest sympathies go out to all his family and friends.

JUNE 23RD

Michael Owen today admitted that he's concerned about his failure to yet get off the mark in Euro 2004 but it would be a foolish punter who doesn't back him to hit the back of the net tomorrow.

As the Liverpool striker has proved in the past, he's at his most dangerous when being written off and he'll be determined to silence his growing army of critics when he lines up in attack against Portugal.

England fans everywhere will have been in particularly good spirits today after watching Germany suffer first round elimination from the tournament after they failed to better Holland's result in their final group game against the classy-looking Czech's.

We shouldn't laugh at the demise of our old foes but remember the World Cup quarter-final of 1970? The World Cup semi-final of 1990? Or the semi-final of Euro '96?

You do? Well, think of all those Germans on

their way home from Portugal tonight and try not to laugh.

Ha! Ha! Ha!

Football can be a cruel game at times but seriously, this is no time to be gloating.

We have much more important items on our agenda, namely a European Championship quarter-final against the host nation in Lisbon tomorrow.

On the eve of the match it's a difficult one to predict. There's no doubt the Portuguese have got stronger as the tournament's progressed but Figo looks a spent force and they possess no real apparent attacking threat.

What they do have in their favour is home advantage and some technically gifted individuals, but whether that's enough to stop the England bandwagon is open for debate.

Fingers crossed it's not!

JUNE 24TH

"After arriving back in blighty following a two week jaunt in Portugal for the first three England games, I feel as though there was a death in the family. How could I not be there for the quarter-final against Portugal? Here I am sitting at my desk with two weeks worth of work to catch up on, but just thinking about slurping a few bottles of superbok with a couple of obligado's thrown in! I have shelved my work for the day and am now planning on booking cheapest flights for the final." - Russell Stander

"It's 9:41 local time in Chicago and the kick-off against Portugal is about 4 hours away. I'm supposed to be working but it's hard to focus. Why is the clock moving so slowly? What time will the lads gather at my house to watch the game? They're all supposed to be working, too but judging by the number of times they've called this morning, there's not a lot of work getting done. Have I ordered the pizza? Do I have enough beer? What are we doing after the game? I've lived in Chicago for 25 years but spent the first 25 years of my life in my native Birmingham, England and I'm an avid Aston Villa fan." - Bill Paul

"It's the morning of England's Quarter Final game with Portugal. I wake up to the radio and immediately think of tonight's game, hoping for an England victory. Suddenly, it's clear - we cannot fail. The weather reporter informs all who are listening that 'today's high will be 19 degrees Centigrade, that's 66 degrees Fahrenheit.' What more of a good luck omen do I need to hear? 1966! Come on England!" - Carl Hughes

"Going into tonight's quarter-final with the hosts, I'm hoping for the best but expecting another schoolboy error around the box which will only serve to make Luton the first scene of domestic Roo-mania. Once we're out, the question on everyone's lips will be if Gazza will hand down the plastic breasts to his young protégé?" - Matt Eccles

"On the day of the big match I get very worried about penalties. I can enjoy a match of 90 minutes and extra time as well if it is needed. I try to understand what a silver goal is and how it is different from a golden goal. But penalties make me come out in a sweat. I hope that all of the England team practise penalties. We don't want them going over the bar!" - James Creighton

Portugal 2 v 2 England
(Portugal win 6-5 on penalties)

Oh no, not again!

The dream is over and the nation is in mourning after England exit another major competition following a dramatic penalty shoot-out.

On what was a roller-coaster of an evening in Lisbon, the ghosts of Turin, Wembley and St Etienne came back to haunt us and poor old Darius Vassell joins an infamous list of England penalty fall guys that includes Chris Waddle, Stuart Pearce, Gareth Southgate and David Batty.

The despair of experiencing defeat in such a manner is becoming a depressingly all too familiar one. And it's not getting any easier to take. In fact, it's getting harder and harder. The truth is, though, it should never have come down to this.

With confidence sky high after the group phase, we went into the titanic quarter-final clash against the hosts with realistic hopes of equalling our best ever performance in the Euro Championships and had it not been for an controversial refereeing decision that ruled out a perfectly legitimate last gasp winner by Sol Campbell we'd have done just that.

The rights and wrongs of Urs Meier's decision will be the subject of heated debate for many years to come but, if we're honest with ourselves, Portugal were the better side. Once Rooney limped off. We retreated into our shell and paid the ultimate price.

The Estadio du Luz is fast becoming our second home and a quick glance around this vast arena prior to kick-off proved as much. We may have been the away team but even the hosts couldn't match the fanaticism of the travelling England fans.

THE FINALS ARRIVE

Over 40,000 gave the boys a raucous welcome and hundreds of St George flags fluttered proudly in the early evening sun.

It was fantastic sight and the locals could only look on in awe. Their response was to bounce up and down in unison but, while it looked impressive, there was a distinct lack of noise. So much for home advantage!

Back to the game itself. It was a nap that Michael Owen would end his Euro 2004 goal drought and when he did it was well worth the wait.

A long hopeful punt up field by James was helped on towards the Portuguese goal by the head of Costinha and an alert Owen seized on a moment of hesitation in the home defence by quickly spinning on a sixpence to hook the ball past the outstretched dive of Ricardo.

It was a typical poacher's effort and one that confirmed our favourite number ten had not lost his touch in front of goal.

Only three minutes had elapsed and boosted by that early strike we comfortably controlled proceedings for the remainder of the half and could even have extended our lead on a number of occasions.

The turning point was the innocuous looking incident that occurred on the half hour mark that forced Rooney, our great white hope, to leave the field clutching his ankle in agony. It was a serious body blow because we'd become so reliant on him and it knocked the wind out of our sails.

The effect his departure was to have on the team was not instantly evident and although we were sitting back a bit more and playing it a bit more cautious Portugal offered little as an attacking force and even when they did threaten to come forward the danger was easily dealt with.

But despite having the luxury of this comfort zone we needed a second goal to tie things up and the longer the game wore on without it the more anxious us fans became.

Our concern became even greater when both Gerrard and Scholes were substituted for the more defence-minded Phil Neville and Owen Hargreaves.

It was an attempt by Sven to tighten things up and hold on for a single goal victory but it was also a sign that invited trouble.

And trouble is what we got. Sensing our apprehension Portugal finally stepped up a gear and seven minutes from time the inevitable happened. Simao crossed from the left and Spurs reject Helder Postiga easily out-jumped John Terry to bury a header into the back of our net.

The home fans finally made themselves heard as the England hordes sat with their heads in their hands. It was a gut-wrenching moment.

With Rooney, Scholes and Gerrard off we looked a pale imitation of the side that had began the game so brightly but with one final throw of the dice in normal time Campbell managed to bundle the ball over the line to score a dramatic winner.

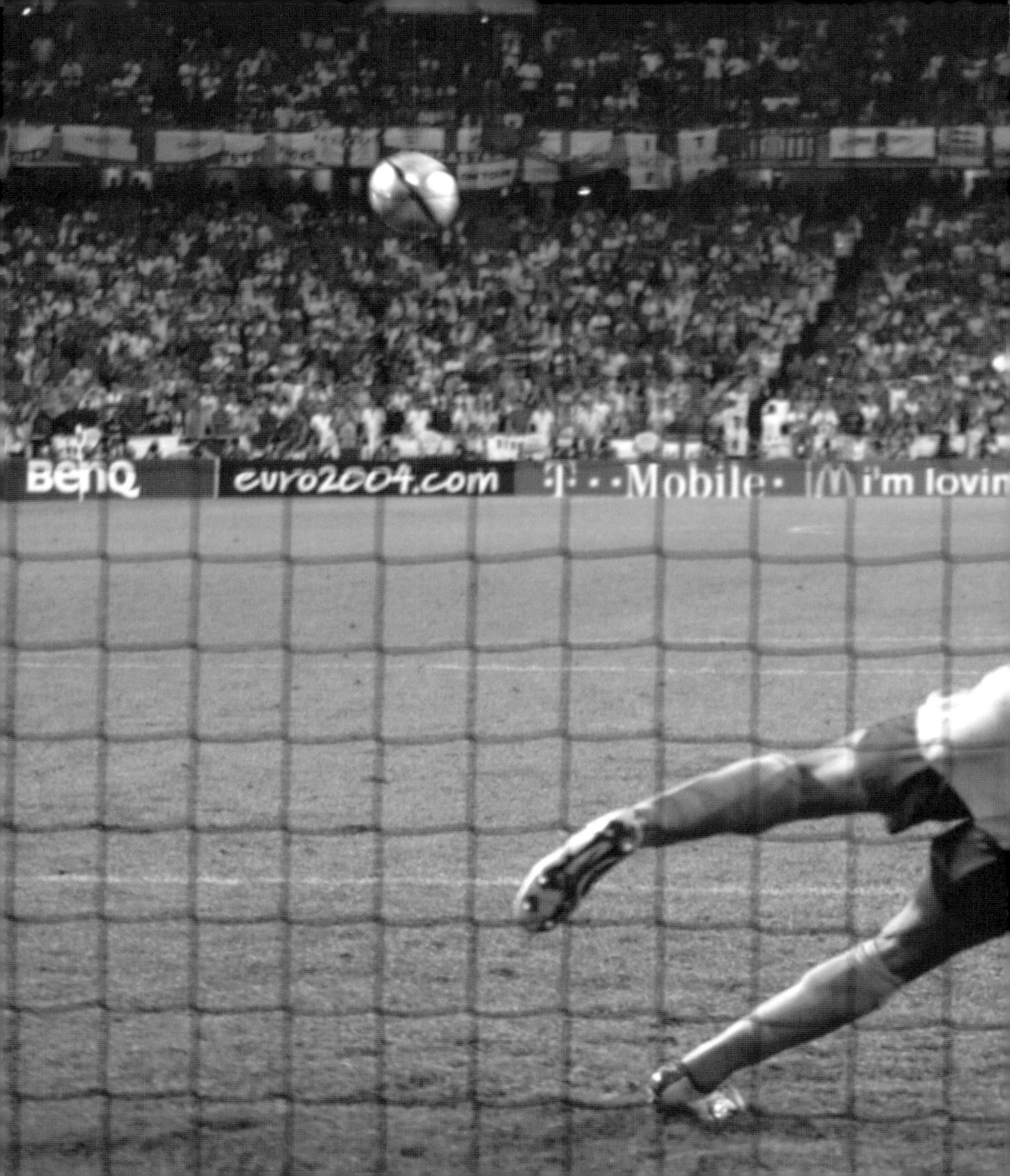

BenQ
euro2004.com
T · · Mobile ·
i'm lovin

Or so we thought.

With the entire nation about to embark on a massive conga Swiss referee Urs Meier promptly disallowed the goal and England's joy was short-lived, much to our anger and frustration.

His reasoning was that Terry had impeded the keeper but television evidence proved he clearly hadn't.

A place in the last four had been snatched from our grasp and the momentum swung in favour of the Portuguese.

As the tie drifted into extra-time both teams tired.

Portugal had also used all three of their substitutes, the last one being the veteran Rui Costa.

But what an inspired substitution by 'Big' Phil Scolari that proved to be.

Ten minutes from the end of the extra half hour Costa advanced towards the edge of the England box before unleashing a venomous shot that flew at 100 miles per hour into the top corner. 2-1 Portugal.

Our Euro dream was fading fast before our very eyes but full credit to the boys, they refused to go down without a fight and five minutes later we were back on our feet celebrating as Lampard hauled us level with a low shot on the turn that left Ricardo rooted to the spot.

That was the last of the scoring from open play. After all that drama, the lottery of a penalty shoot-out would determine the winners of this pulsating tie and that was the cue for even more drama.

First up was Beckham.

Two recent high-profile penalty misses to his name and an undistinguished Euro 2004 about to be etched onto his cv. This was an opportunity for redemption but third time lucky he was not. Incredibly, the ground gave way around the penalty spot as he ran up, forcing him to scuff his effort over the bar and it was advantage Portugal.

Owen and Lampard coolly converted and when Costa blasted wide parity was restored. The tension was unbearable.

Terry and Hargreaves then netted but the selected Portugal players did likewise and now we were into sudden death. Cole scored but so to did Maniche.

At this rate we were never getting to bed. But then up stepped Darius Vassell. He struck his shot well but Ricardo saved superbly.

If Portugal scored their next kick England were out. It was too frightening to watch.

Ricardo dusted himself down and placed the ball on the spot. We turned away but the subsequent roar confirmed what we feared.

The dream was over.

And, not for the first time England was left to drown in a flood of tears.

Player Ratings

David James - 6
Didn't have too much to do but showed some signs of edginess when called upon. Could have done little to stop the two goals.

Gary Neville - 7
Professionalism personified. Another exemplary performance from England's Mr Reliable, who deserves to go further in this tournament.

Ashley Cole - 8
An outstanding display from the Arsenal youngster, both defensively and offensively. Looked a threat when bursting forward, while keeping Ronaldo and Figo quiet all night.

Sol Campbell - 8
Should be a hero tonight, faultless again at the back and can count himself extremely unlucky to have a perfectly legitimate last gasp winner ruled out.

John Terry - 6
Will kick himself for allowing Postiga a free header at goal from which Portugal equalised but shouldn't have been penalised for the part he played in Campbell's disallowed goal.

Steven Gerrard - 6
Not his best game, tired in the second half and was substituted. A disappointing end to a tournament in which he'd promised so much.

Frank Lampard - 7
The pick of our midfield foursome yet again, Lampard was industrious and creative. Never let his head drop and popped up to the score the late equaliser.

David Beckham - 6
Didn't really get into the game. Made no noteworthy contributions, seems to be lacking fitness and should have been substituted instead of Scholes or Gerrard.

Paul Scholes - 6
Showed glimpses of his old self has he carried on where he left off against Croatia. Was surprisingly substituted and it's a decision Sven will regret.

Wayne Rooney - 5
The teenage whizz-kid wasn't on the pitch long enough to have a major impact and if only he hadn't got injured we may have been looking ahead to the semi-final

Michael Owen - 7
Answered his critics in fine style with a well-taken opening goal and took his penalty in the shoot-out with aplomb. Unfortunately, his return to form has come to late and was not enough to keep England in the competition.

Substitutes

Darius Vassell (for Rooney) - 7

Frightened the Portuguese defence with his electric pace but lacked the craft and guile of the man he replaced. Ran his socks off for the cause and should not be blamed for the decisive penalty miss in the shoot-out.

Owen Hargreaves (for Gerrard) - 6

Did what was asked of him when he came on and held his nerve to score from the spot in the shoot-out.

Phil Neville (for Scholes) - 6

Shored up the midfield as he was instructed to do but managed little else of note in the time he was on.

"Okay, so we are on our way home from a major tournament prematurely yet again. But let's not be too harsh on the boys. Apart from the odd player, the team did us proud. We were unlucky to go out on pens and with a bit of luck we could have done it. Luck never seems to go our way in major tournaments but one day it surely will. Keep the faith." - Michael Marks

"Another hard luck story. This country revels in it. There's nothing we like best than a gallant loser! Well, this attitude has to stop because until it does we'll never win anything. Truth is, England were second best to Portugal on the night and went out. It's no good crying about disallowed goals and missed penalties. We're out and deservedly so." - Guy Pease

"England flatter to deceive on the big stage yet again. We really thought it was going to be our year at last but just like at the last World Cup Sven got his tactics wrong and we head home prematurely." - Ste Woods.

"Why, why, why, why? Why can we never ever win on pens? It's become an English trait to choke. Henman does it in the tennis. We nearly did it in the Rugby World Cup and we do it every time in the football. Can we not get these guys to a psychologist beforehand to teach them to be mentally sound for the pens? Look at the Germans, they never lose on pens! They are machines! Come on England — sort it out!" - Mark Thompson

"Too many big name players failed to live up to their huge reputations. That's why we're out of Euro 2004. Don't blame young Darius for his penalty miss. Full credit it to him for having the guts to take it when some of the more experienced players went hiding." - Billy Gee

"It's gone midnight and the tears are still rolling down my face. The dream is over and I'm finding it hard to accept. I was too young to really be affected by the shoot-out defeats against Germany and Argentina in the 90s but now I know how my older brothers felt. Leeds getting relegated last season was bad but this feels worse." - Lyndsey Cookson

Ten days after our elimination from Euro 2004 and the reality hits home that we probably blew our best ever chance of success on foreign soil.

As we sit and watch Greece pull off the biggest shock in the history of a major international football tournament we can only reflect on what might have been.

If only…Wayne Rooney hadn't got injured

If only…We'd have gone for the jugular against Portugal when a goal up

If only…Urs Meier hadn't disallowed Campbell's late goal

If only…the penalty spot hadn't moved

There's no guarantee that we'd have gone on to win the tournament had we beaten Portugal in the quarter-final but the prospect of facing a poor Holland side in the semi's and the rank outsiders from Greece in the final would have had us all realistically dreaming of silverware.

Congratulations to Greece, they fully deserved their triumph and no one can take that away from them but to see the 100/1 outsiders lift that trophy hammered home what a great opportunity we'd wasted.

Had the outstanding Czech Republic side gone on to deservedly lift the trophy then maybe our failure would have been a bit easier to accept, or even France, the pre-tournament favourites and the only side to beat us in open play at Euro 2004.

Alas, it was not to be.

At the end of the day we only made it as far as the last eight and for a nation that entered the tournament with such high expectations and as one of the favourites this simply is not good enough.

Sol's disallowed goal and the dodgy penalty spot will no doubt be put forward has the cause of our exit but the simple fact is we were knocked out prematurely because we lost to a better team on the night.

Sven must hold his hands up and admit that when it mattered most he got it tactically wrong.

And there are certain players, who when they return home and look themselves in the eye will know they could have done better.

But our quarter-final exit apart, Euro 2004, on the whole, was a well-run and enjoyable tournament, helped in no small part by the Portuguese sun, cheap beer and of course Wayne Rooney.

As a consolation prize it was nice to see Rooney, Campbell, Cole and Lampard all named in UEFA's all-star squad.

Each fully deserved the honour. It's just a pity the rest of the England squad didn't aspire to their high standards.

If they had, then this chapter would have been much more upbeat and probably stretched to a few more pages.

Chapter Seven BACK HOME

"Its now the weekend after our exit to Portugal. I returned to England yesterday, having spent a small fortune taking my wife and two sons to the Croatia game and returning with my brother for the Portugal game. Beckham was obviously well below par throughout the whole tournament. His captaincy skills are solely based on leading by example. Therefore, when he is not "doing it", he does not have the character such as Adams, Robson, Pearce etc to grab hold of the players and either demand effort or re-organise if things are obviously not working. Eriksson on the other hand appears to let things plod along hoping that we'll muddle through somehow. Beckham should have been substituted on a number of occasions and the armband handed to Gerrard who, even if he's not on the top of his game, will demand more effort from those around him. Defensive frailties were so obvious to me even during the Croatian game. I am very passionate about England but I will not blindly follow when I see problems. Scolari had the balls to take off Figo when he was off par. We have Sven stating in front of millions on television that Beckham will always be first down on the team sheet. That means that regardless of how ineffective he is, he's in! Take the captaincy off Beckham and get him concentrating on his own game. Then we can start to move forward. Rio will be the voice at the back and Kirkland should be fit for the qualifiers. Give Defoe and Parker a chance. Lets see some small progression instead of 20 substitutes who know that when it comes to the big games, they have a snowballs chance in hell of starting or even being in the squad. England till I die!" - Ian McCrory

"The emergence and success of Wayne Rooney ensured we came out of the tournament with something to be proud of." - Kay Davies

"Its not the first time I've had this feeling of emptiness and despair the morning after an England match, waiting to return back home. In fact I had it in 2000, 1996 and 1992 after watching England falter when they should have done better. Maybe I should have known better - I do now. Blind patriotism, lack of knowledge of foreign football and foreign talent - call it what you want but the expectations are always there, only this time it was different. This time I really believed in Sven and the boys, I sincerely thought that our squad was good enough to go all the way to the final and give the French a run for their money." - Colin Stein

"Sven and the lads were a beacon shining through the dark. Sadly the light was put out by some dubious refereeing decisions! We can hold our heads up high and be proud that we got so far. Roll on the World Cup!" - Ann Harvey

Overall Player Ratings

David James - 6
Made no high-profile blunders of such but hardly instilled us with confidence. Looked vulnerable when under pressure and apart from the odd decent save did nothing to convince us that he should be our long-term number one.

Gary Neville - 8
An inspirational figure at the back, whose experience shone through in every game. Neville led by example and was the reassuring presence when our defence came under pressure. No opposition player got the better of him and he was also effective when pushing forward as an attacking full-back.

Ashley Cole - 8
A major success story. Cole topped a fantastic season at club level with his best performances yet for his country. Caught the eye both defensively and offensively in every game and was one of England's stars.

Sol Campbell - 8
Didn't put a foot wrong all tournament and, just as we predicted, was the rock at the heart of our defence. Returns home with his reputation enhanced and must now be regarded as one of, if not the, top defenders in Europe.

John Terry - 6
Missed the first game through injury and was fortunate to regain his place at the expense of Ledley King. Recovered from a shaky start against the Swiss and improved as the tournament wore on but with Rio Ferdinand's impending return from suspension needed to do a bit more to give Sven a selection headache for the World Cup qualifiers.

Steven Gerrard - 6
A disappointing tournament overall for Gerrard who let talk of a proposed £50 million move to Chelsea affect him and failed to stamp his authority on games like he does for Liverpool.

Played well against Switzerland and Croatia but let us down in the big games v France and Portugal.

Frank Lampard - 8
Grew in stature during the course of the tournament. Was our best midfielder by a mile and must now be considered as one of the first names on Sven's team-sheet.

Weighed in with two important goals and looked very much at home on the big stage.

David Beckham - 5
Four average performances. Lacked fitness and wasn't involved enough in any of the matches.

He'll have to live with the burden of his two missed penalties for a long time to come and he'll be very disappointed with his overall contribution.

Paul Scholes - 6
Started off slowly but showed signs that he was back to his best after the weight of his much-publicised goal drought was removed from his shoulders. Was played out of the position but didn't complain

Wayne Rooney - 9
Our star player without a doubt. England's participation in the tournament would have been a lot duller, and not as long, had it not been for the teenage Scouse striking sensation.

Really came of age during Euro 2004 and unfortunately for Everton fans, now has all the world's top club's chasing after him.

Michael Owen - 6
Looked a pale shadow of his normal self in the opening games and looked to be lacking in confidence after the difficult season he endured at Anfield. Got better as the tournament wore on though and proved he's still a man for the big occasion with the goal against Portugal.

Sadly, his return to form came too late in the day.

Ledley King - 8

Ruturns home with his head held high and reputation enhanced.

Had an outstanding first game against France when he was expected to be given the run around by Henry and co. Was unlucky to lose his place when Terry returned but looks to have a big international future ahead of him.

Emile Heskey - 5

Was only used sparingly and made no real contribution of note.

His participation in this tournament will unfortunately be remembered for conceding THAT free-kick against France.

Some England fans doubted his initial selection in the squad and we saw nothing from the big man to change their mind..

Owen Hargreaves - 5

Solid rather than spectacular, the Bayern Munich man let no one down but failed to convince us that he has the talent to become a regular England international.

Darius Vassell - 6

Should be remembered more for his impact as a substitute against Switzerland than the penalty miss that ultimately cost England the chance of a place in the last four.

But unfortunately, he probably won't. With his electric pace he unsettled opposition defences

when coming into the game late on. Not quite a super sub just yet. But certainly a good sub.

Kieron Dyer - 5

Only saw 15 minutes of action but looked lively and will probably be disappointed not to have figured more, especially in the early games when Scholes failed to shine out on the left side of the midfield.

Phil Neville - 5

A valuable squad player, who can always be relied upon to do a job.

When called upon as a substitute he did just that but didn't show anything that suggests he'd be worthy of a regular place in the starting line-up.

The following squad members played no part at all in the tournament – Wayne Bridge, Paul Robinson, Jamie Carragher, Nicky Butt, Joe Cole and Ian Walker.

Match of the tournament

Contenders:
Sweden 1 v 1 Italy
Czech Republic 3 v 2 Holland
England 4 v 2 Croatia
England 2 v 2 Portugal
Portugal 2 v 1 Holland

Winner: Czech Republic v Holland

England match of the tournament

Contenders:
England 1 v 2 France
England 3 v 0 Switzerland
England 4 v 2 Croatia
England 2 v 2 Portugal

Winner: England v Croatia

England goal of the tournament

Contenders:
Rooney v Switzerland
Gerrard v Switzerland
Rooney v Croatia (1)
Lampard v Croatia
Owen v Portugal

Winner: Owen v Portugal

Villain of the tournament

Contenders:
Emile Heskey
Zinedine Zidane
David Beckham
Urs Meier
Darius Vassell
The penalty spot
Sven

Winner: Urs Meier

Player of the tournament

Contenders:
Milan Baros
Cristiano Ronaldo
Pavel Nedved
Henrik Larsson
Wayne Rooney

Winner: Wayne Rooney

Goal of the tournament

Contenders:
Baros (Czech Republic) v Holland
Costa (Portugal) v England
Maniche (Portugal) v Holland
Larsson (Sweden) v Bulgaria
Ballack (Germany) v Czech Republic

Winner: Maniche

England player of the tournament

Contenders:
Gary Neville
Ashley Cole
Sol Campbell
Frank Lampard
Wayne Rooney

Winner: Wayne Rooney

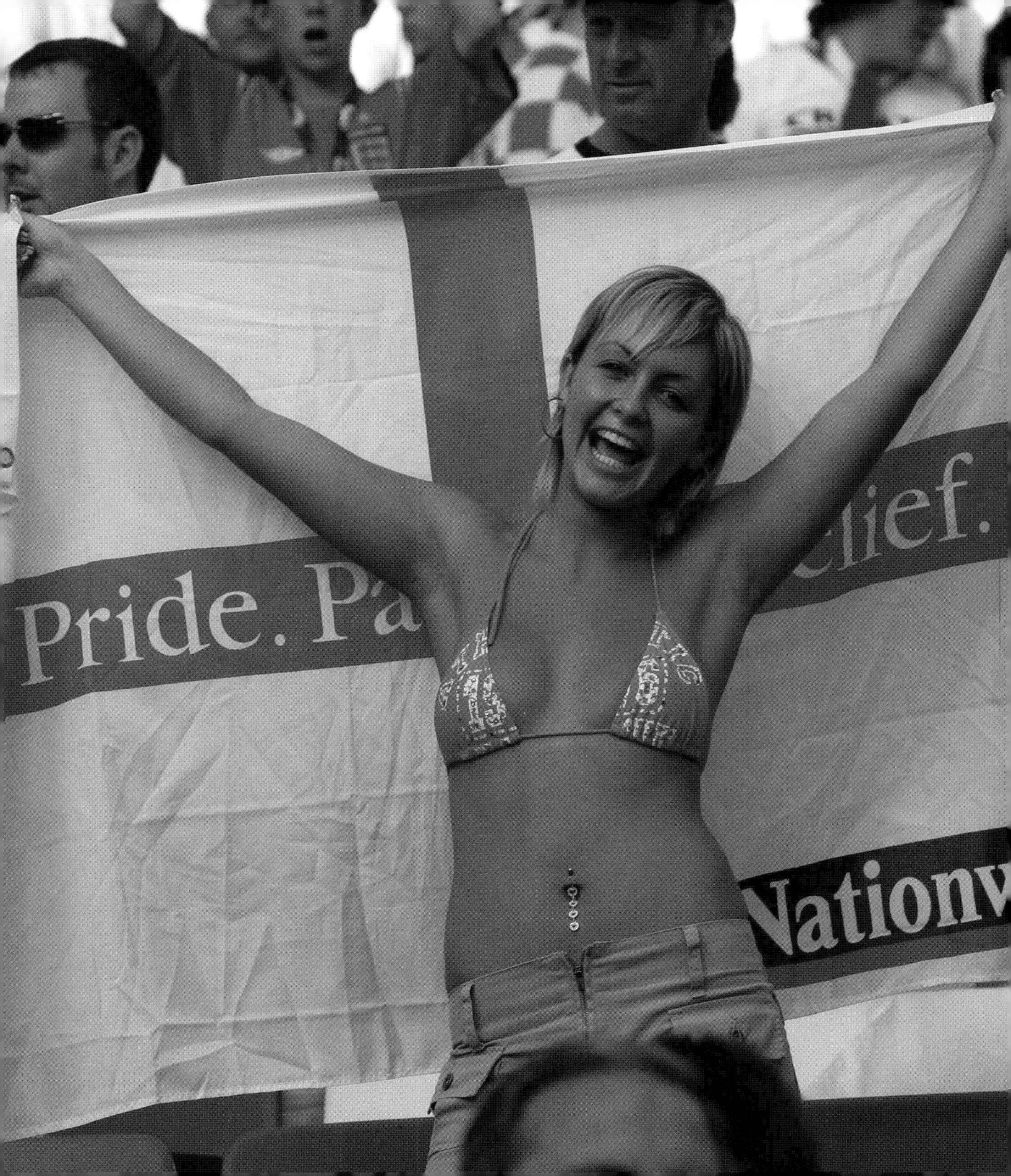
Pride. Pa
elief.
Nationw

Most improved England player

Contenders:
Frank Lampard
Ashley Cole
Ledley King
John Terry

Winner: Frank Lampard

Most exciting team of the tournament

Contenders:
England
Czech Republic
Sweden
France
Portugal

Winner: Czech Republic

Most boring team of the tournament

Contenders:
Russia
Italy
Bulgaria
Switzerland
Latvia
Germany

Winner: Germany

Any tickets for World Cup 2006?

Not surprisingly, the England squad's return to these shores was a low-key one.

It was with a frustrating sense of deja-vu that they touched down back in blighty and there was no open top bus parade, fanfare or street party to greet them.

But the majority of us England fans are eternal optimists. The disappointment of our failure to get beyond the last eight in Portugal is fading fast and already we're looking ahead to the 2006 World in Cup in Germany.

Despite the grumblings of discontent that followed our failure at Euro 2004 there's genuine belief that in two years time we'll be celebrating a first major triumph since '66.

Can you think of a better way to commemorate the 40th anniversary of English football's finest hour?

"Fingers crossed the boy Rooney can continue his remarkable progress. If he does, imagine how good he'll be in 2006? The world beware, that trophy has our name on it and we're coming to get it!"

- Simon Paul

"During my lifetime we've had some of the greatest midfielders in the world - Gazza of course, I remember arguing with someone about Platt being the best in the world at one point. But I've never known us to have 4. Along with the rest of the team, our midfield now picks itself. I don't believe for a minute that there's a better midfield quartet in world football. The question is, why are we not showing it? I do think though that we must be in with a shout for 2006." - Darren Posnack

"I think our squad has a nice variety of players in terms of age, as we can't doubt their quality. We have many young and upcoming players who have a bright future, as well as older, more experienced players like Gary Neville who are good "role-models" for our young players. I felt that we would have won Euro 2004, but unfortunately it wasn't meant to be. We look a good side for World Cup 2006 though and I know we'll do well and win. COME ON ENGLAND!" - Harshil Parekh

"Once again, England have fallen short of the mark. Pre-tournament promise ending in bitter disappointment. It has been proved once again that negative defensive football with a slender one-goal lead is tactical suicide. Praise must be given to the defence for the manner in which they held a relentless Portugal at bay for 83 minutes, especially the superb Sol Campbell. Darius Vassell must not be made a scapegoat of a wonderful penalty save. We had the desire and the determination, but unfortunatly not the luck. World Cup 2006, 40 years on, must surely be England's year?" - Michael Jarrett

"How's this for true passion? I've been to about 15 England away matches, and I've never had any money! My first tournament was Euro '88 in Germany. I slept in a park and we lost every game, but I was hooked. I missed Italia '90 as I had my finals to take! But I was in Sweden for Euro '92. Again, I was skint. Again, I slept rough, and again, England could not win. I managed to find work, a place to live, and a girl. I stayed three months! I went to Holland in '93 for a crucial World Cup qualifier. We lost, and didn't make it to USA '94. I was gutted, so I went back to Sweden! In '97 I hitchhiked to Poland with a fiver in my pocket for another crucial World Cup qualifier. This time we won! I finally got to a World Cup in France '98. I also made it to Japan in 2002. Again, I found work, and a girl...Now I'm looking forward to Germany in 2006!"

- Jim Pedley

"In Lisbon on semi final day having a few beers in this restaurant right over the road from the Alvalade stadium and there was just Portuguese fans inside and out. There was no Dutch fans anywhere. Then out of nowhere this bright orange double decker bus came driving past at about 2 miles an hour followed by all of the Dutch fans, each one dressed from head to toe in orange, all marching up together, the whole road was just like an orange river. There was a brass band with them and they stopped right outside the restaurant we were in. As they were playing a tune they started playing it slower and slower and slower and as they got slower they got lower (as did all the fans around them) until they were all lay in the middle of the road playing this tune really, really slowly. Then they started speeding up and they all started to rise up again until they got back to full speed at which point everyone started jumping up and down singing. Everyone in the restaurant fell about in fits of laughter!" - James Foster

Thanks to every fan who contributed to the production of Pride. Passion. Belief. Without your help it would not have been possible. Here is a selection of some more emails that were submitted to us during the course of the tournament.

"Throughout my life I have had dreams of living abroad and last year I got to achieve that ambition. I now live deep in the heart of Texas. But whenever I dreamed about going away from England, my thoughts always came back to football and particularly to my home team Port Vale. I have always loved to watch England play and have seen international competitions in the past whilst on holiday abroad in Europe. But coming to the States is another world. It is not so bad these days, but it is still a pretty uncultivated field when it comes to football -soccer as they insist on calling it. For the past few weeks I have been following the build-up to Euro 2004 and pondering as to how and where I was going to watch my team. I have my shirt and my flag and all the other stuff that help to make the day, but the options for watching the game are not as I would like. I either have to pay $20 a game to watch the coverage on TV or go to one of those few pubs that show sports other than baseball. I found a "British" pub called the Londoner in Dallas, but they too are charging $20 (apparently due to extortionate fees charged by the satellite company). So I decided to stay at home and pay the money. So I made some tea, sat on the sofa with my dog and prepared for the game. I get used to the lack of atmosphere these days, listening as I do to internet radio broadcasts of Port Vale matches every Saturday during the season. But this is special. The teams come out and I stand as they play the British national anthem. The whistle blows and I am almost there. In the end, there is no difference now. I could be sitting in England or here in Texas, but I support my country. Come on England!" - Tony Boulton

"The whole experience was excellent. Before going out there we harboured concerns about whether there would be trouble makers spoiling it for everybody else but once we arrived in Portugal you couldn't fault the atmosphere." - JJ

"They say a team without fans is like a nation without hope!!! And that is why the English football team stands strong because of the high support from the fans. Thank you fans, the English team wouldn't have made it without you; thank you the English team for making the fans proud" - Collins Dokubo Owen

"I went to Lisbon Portugal for three days to watch England V France what a weekend everything was so perfect until injury time - if only they just held it and kept kicking the ball out of play, and of course Beckham scored that penalty. But it was the best football weekend ever! Better than West Ham going to Cardiff for the Playoff Final 2004. I now hope England go to World Cup 2006 - I will surly get tickets and stay in Germany until England, God willing, lift that World Cup for the 2nd time. 1966 — 2006." - G Sing

"The passion, the power, the goosebumps, the hairs standing on end, that very moment when everyone stands to their feet, surrounded by people wearing the self same top as you; hundreds, no, thousands of people all willing eleven men on from the soles of their feet to the ends of the longest hairs on their heads. The pride and the pain of the 90 minutes that stands before each and every one of you. It doesn't matter what you earn, what car you drive, the colour of your skin or the language you choose to speak; for those ninety or so minutes ahead you and tens of thousands of others all want exactly the same thing. Whether it's Beckham slotting the perfect cross onto the head of Mickey Owen; Rooney going on one of his, if not glamorous, or beautiful, "dazzling" runs into the opposition box; Lamps cracking one form thirty yards or Campbell climbing at the far past in the last second to score the winner. It's the pride, the passion and the belief that make watching England better than any drug, any other event or life defining moment, any prize, any loss... better than anything! It's the buzz of those people that you nodded at as you took your seat turning and hugging you. Strangers but for the colours of your shirts. That is what makes watching England special." - Jon Harvey

"My son Neil and seven of his friends are staying at Praya del Rey for the whole tournament. He rang after the disappointment against France. He said if their was going to be any trouble it would have been that night, but they shook hands with French and went back to the villa to drown their sorrows. Although it is not going to happen I feel the media should focus on the fans going to the games because these are the football fans of England who make me feel so proud. They have outnumbered the opposing fans at both games so far. They have paid out a lot of money to be there, which proves how passionate they are. I, as a staunch England fan, salute every fan at the games." - Neil's dad

"I'm still in touch with a Portugal fan that we met in a bar next to the Alvalade on the afternoon of the Portugal v Holland game. We had a few beers with him and his friend (1 Benfica fan and 1 Sporting fan!). They then they escorted us to the ground and on the way we joined them in smoking a lucky cigar 'you smoke and Portugal will win,' they told us! As we went into the ground they told us that they would take us to the best parties in Lisbon afterwards if Portugal did in fact win. After the game we didn't think anything of it and started our journey back to the Algarve when he rang my mobile asking where we were and were we ready to go and party! He was very disappointed when I told him we had set off back to the Algarve, but we've got an open invitation to go over for the Lisbon derby any time." - Robert

"England fans have, in the past gained a fair amount of notoriety for their misdemeanours outside of grounds following the disappointments on the pitch. However, after a concerted effort by the powers that be to clean up this aspect of our beautiful game, we as a nation can now be rightly proud, not only of the boys on the pitch who are doing the business but also the dedicated army of fans who follow the team everywhere. Euro 2004 has highlighted these fans and the wonderful support they give the team, making us possibly the best-supported nation (yes I'm including the home nation in that statement) in the whole tournament. Not being one of the lucky ones who managed to get tickets, it has been truly heart-warming to see on TV the fans getting behind the team and giving them the support that their efforts well and truly deserve. I'm sure all of us wish to be at the tournament rather than watching the games on a screen in a packed pub, not only to watch the game first hand, but to be part of those celebrations." - Michael Heales

"We were based on the Algarve and drove up to Lisbon for the Croatia and Portugal games and also for the Portugal v Holland semi. England match days were just awesome from start to finish. 90% of the traffic on the motorway from the Algarve to Lisbon was England fans and the employees of the toll booths must have dreaded it, especially after the Croatia game when at 1am the queue for each booth must have been a dozen cars deep, each car beeping it's horn until they had passed through!" - Rob Dolphin

"Ricky Butcher of Eastenders fame (real name Syd Owen) walks into the square and doesn't let on to calls of 'Riiickkky' Bianca style. On his way back out I shout 'Alright Sid' and he lets on with thumbs up and cheesy grin!" - Jamie Foster

"One of my abiding memories of our visit to Portugal for the Euro 2004 finals would have to be the supermarket manager at the Centro Colombo mall over the road from the Stadium of Light. We went in and bought some warm beers off the shelf and as we left the store he had a huge plastic trolley full of crushed ice. They were bagging it up and giving it to the football fans for their beers. Everybody was made up and so was he because as I pointed out to him that the colder the beers, the quicker we drink them and the more we buy. The beaming smile on his face suggested he'd just won the lottery!" - Simon Eland

"Swathed in the Cross of St George, as modern knights of the Lionheart's Crusade. Stout John and Joan Bulls revelling in their moment with vino sated smiles. Lads and chaps and blokes, and best still, lasses and dollies and birds so burnished and browned, like the sandals of the fishermen of the peninsular. All cheeky and chubby and cherubic, just there for their time to shine. Another World from the grit and drizzle of Merseyside; the puke-streaked avenues of the Black Country and the cash-coke-chic of the hard Capital, these provincial hordes are united, untied and liberated by Ozone and the flavour of Iberia. You know, a pure thread runs through the heart of each of we travelling England fans. It is the fine, silken twines of Hope and Glory. The Three Lions' fans are singular and unique. We are the World's greatest football fans. Ever. We are revered for our loyalty and terrace-tenor-harmony; feared for the ferocity of our belief and courted for our dipsomania and gustatorial excesses." - Philip Glaister

FANS EMAILS AND PICS

"My family and I are passionate about our national team. So much so that we put two St George Cross flags with the three Lions emblem on our car and have walked around in England clothing for most of the tournament. So what? I hear you cry, well the fact of the matter is that we live in Wales, my wife is Welsh and my kids have all been born in Wales, but that hasn't stopped them from being proud of their English heritage and, in my wife's case, proud to be British and have a team at the championships. We have had some excellent banter whilst on the road, we've had the patriotic Welsh booing, giving the thumbs down, shouting Wales, Thierry Henry and Zinedine Zidane. On the other side of the coin we have had the English contingent in this part of Wales flashing their lights and sounding their horns, leaning out of the windows and waving flags of their own. I have even had a van pull up alongside me with a guy virtually hanging out of the window shouting in the thickest Welsh accent 'can I buy one of your flags, I'll give you a fiver'. After saying 'I couldn't sell, it'll be like selling one of the kids,' he shouted 'seven fifty I'll give you seven fifty,' obviously I refused again but shouted back where he could get hold of one for four quid. It only goes to show the character of people once barriers are somehow broken, I suggest we all put flags on our cars, even if there isn't a tournament, it'll certainly be a fight against road rage." - Paul Bridges

"Being female and blonde, my fella thinks I'm too thick to understand football. Maybe I don't understand the offside rule and all that, but I do like a good game. All the excitement leading up to Euro 2004 was electric and now it's here I'm loving it. Lastly, where is Robbie Fowler? I love fowler and miss him. Bring back Fowler." - Karen McCrudden

"My family and I are passionate about our national team. So much so that we put two St George Cross flags with the three Lions emblem on our car and have walked around in England clothing for most of the tournament. So what? I hear you cry, well the fact of the matter is that we live in Wales, my wife is Welsh and my kids have all been born in Wales, but that hasn't stopped them from being proud of their English heritage and, in my wife's case, proud to be British and have a team at the championships. We have had some excellent banter whilst on the road, we've had the patriotic Welsh booing, giving the thumbs down, shouting Wales, Thierry Henry and Zinedine Zidane. On the other side of the coin we have had the English contingent in this part of Wales flashing their lights and sounding their horns, leaning out of the windows and waving flags of their own. I have even had a van pull up alongside me with a guy virtually hanging out of the window shouting in the thickest Welsh accent 'can I buy one of your flags, I'll give you a fiver'. After saying 'I couldn't sell, it'll be like selling one of the kids,' he shouted 'seven fifty I'll give you seven fifty,' obviously I refused again but shouted back where he could get hold of one for four quid. It only goes to show the character of people once barriers are somehow broken, I suggest we all put flags on our cars, even if there isn't a tournament, it'll certainly be a fight against road rage." - Paul Bridges